ANIME
ARCHITECTURE

ANIME ARCHITECTURE

IMAGINED WORLDS AND
ENDLESS MEGACITIES

Stefan Riekeles

With 386 illustrations

Contents

INTRODUCTION
6–17

AKIRA
18–55

PATLABOR: THE MOVIE
56–67

PATLABOR 2: THE MOVIE
68–91

GHOST IN THE SHELL
92–135

METROPOLIS
136–157

INNOCENCE
158–185

TEKKONKINKREET
186–221

REBUILD OF EVANGELION
222–249

GLOSSARY & BIOGRAPHIES
250–256

INTRODUCTION

This publication presents the meticulously crafted architecture and cityscapes created for some of the most influential science-fiction anime films produced from the 1980s to the early 2000s. Since the huge success of *AKIRA* (1988) and *Ghost in the Shell* (1995), many Japanese anime have been counted as landmarks in global pop culture. The genre has long had an enormous cultural influence in Japan, and now also has a rapidly growing global audience – international cinema, music and fashion all regularly refer to its characters and stories. Anime conventions – gatherings of several thousand fans, many of them dressed up as their favourite characters – are held every month the world over. In recent decades, anime has established itself as a powerful medium for creating, catalysing and synthesizing a wide range of trends in pop culture, and its universe covers an incredibly diverse range of themes, specialities and fetishes.

Although depictions of future cityscapes, with their various reconceptions of urban architecture, represent only a small part of the anime universe, these images have had a decisive influence on what we think of nowadays as the genre's typical style. Alongside the story and the dialogue, the background artwork in anime reveals the 'world view' that the artists are aiming to express. The director Mamoru Oshii articulated this when he said: 'Over the years, I've come to realize that the silent world behind the characters is where the director has to communicate his core vision. The drama is just the surface of the film. The backgrounds are the director's vision of reality' (Oshii 2004b, p. 120). All the artworks featured in this volume present highly diverse visions of future cities – how these visions relate to our existing urban environment is indicative of each artist's intention.

The technologically advanced futures presented in this book have often been created by the surprisingly traditional means of pencil, paint and paper. This contrast between the message conveyed by an image and the techniques used in its creation was a great source of inspiration when compiling this overview. The works all stem from the period between 1988 and 2010, a time during which the anime industry changed significantly as a result of the introduction of digital technologies. Over these twenty-two years, paper-based background artwork reached its peak in terms of both realism and dedication to detail. Nowadays, computer animation is used in all areas of production, but the most important tools for the creators of the works featured here still include the layout table, paper, pencil and paintbrush – these artists established their careers and reputations at a time when anime was almost exclusively hand-drawn on paper.

Need Kajima, #1
Shuichi Kusamori
Digital illustration, *detail*

However, 'hand-drawn' is not a valid criterion when distinguishing these works from digital artworks. The latter are also hand-drawn, but the hand moves a digital brush instead of the traditional wooden shaft with bristles. The scope of this book, therefore, is to present paper-based works, painted with wet colour, drawn with pencils or photographed on film. It is the author's fascination for paper and paint, for tangible materials, that has inspired the selection of illustrations. Only feature films that have had a theatrical release and were produced with specific attention to the background artwork have been considered. Most anime productions are intended for television release. However, because the big screen demands more detail, the increased budget and time allocated to background work for these theatrical releases allow for more intricate illustrations. This provides the opportunity for art departments to excel in their domain, and therefore to produce outstanding artwork.

Even with these criteria, this overview suffers from the absence of some important individuals. There are three names that should be mentioned specifically. The works of Hayao Miyazaki, which all feature exquisite background artwork, have not been considered because they do not represent future cityscapes but instead build a universe that is unique to themselves, and merit consideration in a separate volume. The imagery of Makoto Shinkai's films is a passionate yet contemporary continuation of the artwork presented here, and that is also the reason why I did not include it – Shinkai and his colleagues belong to the post-paper era, and thus will have to be showcased somewhere else. Sadly, the works of Satoshi Kon could not be included, although all of his films depict Tokyo from a more or less futuristic perspective. The main reason for this omission is that Kon's archive is not yet ready to be published, and thus access was difficult.

Rather than concentrating on the final product, the research for this publication focused on the drawings that precede the cinematic image, as these reveal highly inventive and individual artistic achievements that are not always immediately obvious from the picture we see on the screen. Many artists and studios generously supplied illustrations from different phases of the production process, some of which had been published before. However, in most previous publications the edges of sheets were trimmed; the sheets had often not been scanned in their entirety; and the resolution of these existing scans was usually not sufficient. This project focuses on the paper-based nature of these illustrations, therefore all of the final production backgrounds and layouts have been scanned again specifically for the purpose of this publication.

The complicated process of collecting the illustrations shaped this undertaking from the start. In most cases, the artists work for production studios as employees, and thus cede the rights in their work wholly to their employers. Even if one manages to locate a drawing, there is still a long way to go in order to obtain permission to publish it. In addition, in everyday studio practice these artworks are rarely seen as valuable – in a commercial context, all that matters ultimately is the final product, the animated film. It is often unclear what ends up happening to these materials. In most cases, it would seem that they are simply discarded at the end of the production. Although artifacts from anime production are often bought and sold by those within the fan culture, sometimes in specialized shops, such transactions generally involve cels – the painted sheets of film seen on the cinema screen. These belong to the last stage of the production process, and are rarely executed by the people who make the creative decisions.

Access to the illustrations was possible thanks to our previous efforts in the same sphere. Research for this undertaking began in the year 2008, and the first public presentation came three years later with the travelling exhibition 'Proto Anime Cut' (Les Jardins des Pilotes 2011–13) and its accompanying publication *Proto Anime Cut Archive* (Riekeles 2011). The second instalment was the exhibition 'Anime Architecture' (Les Jardins des Pilotes 2016–). The present publication is highly unusual in making the illustrations that form the basis for the cinematic experience of anime available to a wide audience for close inspection. Pictures that only appear for seconds on the screen can now be studied in great detail.

The Production Process

The production of anime is a collaborative process involving concept developers, narrators, drafters and animators. They usually work in a strictly organized and industrialized system, which I will outline below.

Settings, Layouts and Backgrounds

If we were to classify the illustrations reproduced in this book in terms of the production processes that films shot with live actors on a studio set employ, most would have been originated by the production-design department. The job of a production designer is to invent the universe in which the director wishes to locate the film. In the development stage, the film architect – as the production designer is sometimes called – will try to provide a set that can accommodate different camera perspectives, allowing the whole scene to be shot there. In Japanese, the expression *sekai-kan* (which can be literally translated as 'world view') is used to describe the function of production design – to create worlds. In anime, these worlds are created through a cinematic montage of graphics and paintings. In principle, any visual fantasy could be realized by these methods. However, to make a story convincing and to transform the characters into figures with whom we can identify, the drawn and painted architecture has to harmonize with the world of the film – it must be credible in narrative terms.

There are three stages that precede the creation of the completed background picture, which will then be photographed or scanned for the animation to take place: the setting, the image board and the layout.

The first stage is the setting, otherwise known as the concept design. For every scene, a concept is required in which the basic elements of the film's world are depicted. The setting consists of a number of pencil drawings that combine to illustrate the scene of the action for the benefit of the director and the background painters. The architectural style and the landscape are defined, the workings of mechanical elements such as vehicles or weapons are elucidated, and the physical appearance and characteristic poses of the main figures are developed. Settings are created by the art department in close collaboration with the director, and the drawings themselves are usually executed by the layout designer or the art director.

The second stage in creating an anime world is the artboard or image board of a particular scene, painted in colour. Several versions are usually made that depict different seasons or times of day. Through the image board, the art director indicates a colour palette for the background painters to use.

Need Kajima
Concept design
Shuichi Kusamori
Pencil on paper
24.8 × 35 cm (9⅞ × 13⅞ in.)

In 2007, art director Shuichi Kusamori was commissioned to produce an illustration for use in an advertising campaign for Kajima Corporation, one of the largest construction companies in Japan. The firm builds high-rise structures, railways, power plants, dams and bridges – the sort of infrastructure that features prominently in so many science-fiction anime. Kusamori received this assignment after working as art director for *Metropolis* (2001) and *Innocence* (2004).

    Kusamori's work suggests the mutual dependence of technology, urban visions and fantasy worlds in anime films. While some illustrations presented in this volume draw directly on existing realities, others are hand-drawn or computer-generated fantasies, even if they may perhaps become achievable one day thanks to developments in construction materials and methods. In his design for the future of Kajima, Kusamori blends the cinematic visions of science-fiction anime with the real-estate projects under construction by the company.

The final phase required before the background can be painted is the layout. A scene generally consists of several takes, which are also called 'cuts' in anime terminology. In animation, the editing has already been finished in the storyboard phase, thus the term 'cut' does not refer to a transition between one shot and the next, as in live-action film, but to the shot itself. One layout is required per cut. The composition of the film image is defined in this line drawing, which contains precise details on the background, on the position of the figures and other moving objects, on the perspective and on camera movements. There are few people who can draw the distorted perspective of a camera lens, and it is particularly difficult to render the effects of a wide-angle lens. Takashi Watabe – whose work is featured extensively in this publication – is one of those artists (Oshii 1995b).

Alongside the image board, the layout is used as the blueprint for the art director when creating the final production background. Because most of the illustrations presented in this book stem from this phase of film production, the role of the art director will be introduced in more detail in the next section. However, it is important to keep in mind that each illustration presented in this volume is just one stage in a long process of incremental steps.

Art Directors

The art director supervises the artwork of the film. This artwork includes all that is visible in the background behind the characters. Working alongside the director, an art director develops the world of the anime film, in which the characters exist and the dramas are spun. In addition, art directors often draw final production backgrounds themselves, while also overseeing the quality of those background images drawn by the background-art staff.

When the artists featured in this volume entered the anime industry, there was no dedicated education programme for becoming an anime art director. Most of the skills had to be learned on the job in a production studio. When it came to training up-and-coming talents in the art of background painting, one of the most important studio workshops was Kobayashi Production. Founded in 1968 by Shichiro Kobayashi, the company specialized in the production of background art for animation until its closure in 2011. A great number of art directors learned their profession under the supervision and guidance of Kobayashi, who was a leading figure in the industry. He was extremely influential in creating the characteristic style of anime, having studied classical painting at the Musashino Art University in Tokyo before joining the Toei Doga studio in 1966. In 1968, he left to found his own studio, and went on to be the art director on numerous important anime series and films, including *Dokonjo Gaeru* (1972–74), *Lupin III: The Castle of Cagliostro* (1979), *Ashita no Joe 2* (1981), *Magical Angel Creamy Mami* (1983), *Golgo 13: The Professional* (1983), *Urusei Yatsura 2: Beautiful Dreamer* (1984) and *Revolutionary Girl Utena* (1997).

Kobayashi Production started its operations at a moment when the Japanese animation industry was entering a phase of rapid growth. Art directors of the 'Kobayashi School' have since created some of the most successful anime series and films, many of which are considered milestones in global pop culture. A number of these artists went on to run their own studios after they left the firm. The apprentices at Kobayashi Production whose work is featured in this volume are Shinji Kimura, Hiromasa Ogura, Hiroshi Ono and Toshiharu Mizutani. Kazuo Oga, famous for his work with Hayao Miyazaki, also started his career there. Every time I ask these artists about their time at Kobayashi, their eyes light up at the memory. In addition, a number of influential art directors were educated at Nippon Animation, where Nizo Yamamoto and Shuichi Kusamori established their reputations. The latter studied under Masahiro Ioka, famous for his work on *Heidi: Girl of the Alps* (1974).

Films and Methods

Between 1988 and 2010, both the artistic skills and the profiles of the creators featured in this publication increased rapidly, as did the use of technology in the anime production process. One reason that these artists have been directly involved in the creation of this book is to ensure that the development of their specific styles over time is captured. To this end, the artworks are presented in chronological order, reflecting the year in which each project was produced.

All of the artists presented share a common interest in the realistic construction of possible world views, and in creating convincing visions of future cities and landscapes. Although this kind of realism is just one of the infinite possible styles in animation, it has helped to define the specific qualities of anime as a unique form of cinematic expression. The first anime to achieve an almost cine-realistic style was *Royal Space Force: The Wings of Honneamise* (1987), directed by Hiroyuki Yamaga. Several of the artists presented in this volume worked on *Royal Space Force* in the early stages of their careers: Hiromasa Ogura served as the art director; Hideaki Anno directed the animation and is credited as special-effects artist; and Takashi Watabe worked on the layouts. Unfortunately the film did not really catch the attention of audiences at the time of its release because it was rapidly overshadowed by *AKIRA* (1988), but it now enjoys a significant cult following.

AKIRA started the global boom in anime. For much of its audience, this was the first animated film that they perceived as specifically Japanese in both origin and style. The story's location, Neo Tokyo, employs the dialectic of centre and periphery, and also the compelling motif of a high-rise tower that extends deep underground through its systems of pipes and sewers. Its multi-layered and densely embroidered cityscape draws inspiration from Fritz Lang's *Metropolis* (1927) and Ridley Scott's *Blade Runner* (1982), as well as the urban visions of Japanese architect Kenzo Tange. The film was almost entirely produced on paper. Although some digital effects were incorporated during post-production, all the background artworks were painted in poster colour and subsequently shot on film. As a visual tour de force, *AKIRA* had a tremendous influence on the subsequent expectations of film enthusiasts, and on understandings of what anime could be.

With his Patlabor films – *Patlabor: The Movie* (1989) and *Patlabor 2: The Movie* (1993) – Mamoru Oshii took a different approach. Instead of relying on the dystopian visions of *Blade Runner* and *Metropolis*, Oshii grounded his cinematic vision on detailed, carefully elaborated cityscapes based around the realities of contemporary Tokyo. Oshii trusts in location-hunting more than futuristic architecture when creating cinematic universes, thus *Patlabor 2: The Movie* was the first anime to depict Tokyo in cine-realistic images. The film's extraordinarily sober impression was based on intense layout work that aimed to achieve a convincing emulation of live-action films.

Oshii's work during this paper-based period culminated in *Ghost in the Shell* (1995), which is considered the second cornerstone of sci-fi anime, alongside *AKIRA*. The project contained eight minutes and twenty-seven seconds of digital footage, and is regarded as a pinnacle in the art of background painting (Oshii 1995b). In contrast, Rintaro's *Metropolis* (2001), Oshii's sequel to *Ghost in the Shell, Innocence* (2004) and Michael Arias's *Tekkonkinkreet* (2006) were all created using hybrid workflows. These projects mark transition points in the transformation of anime from paper-based to digital, with both means of production coexisting. Large parts of their designs were painted on paper then integrated into a digital production system.

The eponymous city in *Metropolis*, for instance, is made up of two layers, the lower and the higher city, corresponding with Lang's original vision. The higher city's architecture is digitally rendered, while the lower city's caverns and infrastructure are painted in poster colour on paper. In this way, the producers did not aim to integrate paper-based and digital animation, but used both means of film-making to establish distinguishable aesthetics for different parts of the cityscape.

The urban setting of *Innocence* is more abstracted than the city seen in *Ghost in the Shell*. The production is a milestone in the digitalization of the animation process, seamlessly combining 2D and 3D computer-generated animation techniques (these are usually simply referred to as 2DCG and 3DCG, and these abbreviations will be used in this book), and the rendering of the cityscape in the film is of outstanding quality. Throughout the project, Oshii explored the changing possibilities of the art department, encouraging his staff to rethink and redesign the role of the art director (Oshii 2004b, p. 118).

Tekkonkinkreet was planned as a completely computer-animated film. However, most of the animation work ended up being done on paper. At Studio 4°C, Arias found drafters that he considered 'to be the best character animators in the world' and he wanted them to work with tools that they already knew well, that is pencil and paper. Instead of setting the film amid the neon lights and gloom of a *Blade Runner*-like world, the artists drew much of their inspiration from Kichijoji, the area of Tokyo in which Studio 4°C operates. For *Tekkonkinkreet*, Arias favoured a documentary-style handheld camera over the perfect compositions that anchor most traditional animation projects. This directing strategy presented an artistic and technical challenge, which was solved through a hybrid production with paper-based background paintings that were then composited onto a 3DCG model of the environment.

For the *Rebuild of Evangelion* series, which began in 2007, all artwork was created digitally, with only layouts and concept designs remaining paper-based. Its director, Hideaki Anno, shares the fascination for urban infrastructure – the nerve centres and neuralgic points of the modern city – felt by fellow directors Katsuhiro Otomo and Mamoru Oshii. However, he has little apparent interest in adopting 'cyberpunk' stylings for his cityscapes. Anno's designs are influenced by another medium – the miniature sets of tokusatsu films. Tokusatsu is a term denoting live-action films with stories that revolve around a series of special-effects shots. The best-known Japanese examples are monster films such as *Godzilla* (1954), directed by Ishiro Honda, and the superhero TV series *Ultraman* (1966–67), directed by Hajime Tsuburaya and Akio Jissoji. The sets for these projects were made in miniature, and form an arena for a battle between good and evil. Anno is 'more impressed by a miniature that looks exactly like a real scene than by the real scene itself' (Anno 2008, p. 452), and drew his layouts of the cityscape for *Rebuild of Evangelion* with the idea of tokusatsu in mind. These layouts were the last step in the production process drawn with pencil on paper: all subsequent

Need Kajima, #2
Shuichi Kusamori
Digital illustration

steps were executed digitally. Therefore, parts of these layouts are sometimes void of any information, merely specifying that these particular areas should be drawn later in 3DCG – these empty spots forecast the end of the paper-based era.

Acknowledgments
This volume is a collaborative effort, just like the many drawings and works presented within it. I'm deeply indebted to all the artists and studio staff who have allowed me to compile this book as a resource for anybody who is interested in the art and craft behind the complex world views of anime.

I would like to extend my sincerest gratitude to the artists whose works are the foundation of this publication, to which they all contributed generously. I thank Hideaki Anno for providing such unprecedented access to his rare original drawings and photographs; Michael Arias for an insightful meeting in Berlin and for his subsequent support of the task of publishing the works of Shinji Kimura; Haruhiko Higami for kindly providing his prints and also for his insights into his collaborations with Mamoru Oshii; Shinji Kimura for a long afternoon at Studio 4°C, and for his detailed description of his work; Shuichi Kusamori and his wife Yoshiko Kusamori for several meetings, and for scanning all his work once more; Toshiharu Mizutani for an inspiring afternoon at his studio, for his account of his work on *AKIRA* and for scanning his illustrations again; Kazuo Oga for a wonderful evening with Hiromasa Ogura and for his deep insights into his time at Kobayashi Production; Hiromasa Ogura for always warmly welcoming me into his studio, for his camaraderie and for his continued support of this project since its very beginning; Hiroshi Ono for the great visit to his studio and for scanning many illustrations; Mamoru Oshii for his fascinating insights into his work, and his continued support of the project; Katsuhiro Otomo for granting permission for this rare opportunity to publish the background artwork of his masterpiece *AKIRA*; and Takashi Watabe for a fascinating journey into his personal universe, and a look behind the scenes of animation production design.

Defining the scope and range of this publication would not have been possible without the advice of several experts in the field. I am very grateful to Ryusuke Hikawa, who played a critical role in its preparation and research, time and again improving the quality of my work with his inexhaustible knowledge and comprehensive archives. Many aspects of this publication are informed by his research, and without his insights the project simply wouldn't have had the same depth. Many thanks also to Keiji Naito for his great help in locating the original drawings for *AKIRA* and for a productive afternoon at the archives of Kodansha. At Niigata University, Joon Yang Kim was a great help, and established our contact with Gainax. Although we could not finally include the illustrations for *Royal Space Force*, this relationship was extremely helpful in shaping the contents of this book. Kaichiro Morikawa spent a Sunday afternoon with me in his office explaining his work and sharing his insights, for which many thanks. Kan Miyoshi was a great support in the work with Studio Khara, and spent a full afternoon with Mr Hikawa and myself at the offices of ATAC to teach me the basics of tokusatsu. Toshio Yabe's insights about urbanism in anime, especially in Oshii's work, were very informative. Nae Morita was a great help in tracking down the archives of *Royal Space Force*, and gave me a greater understanding of the relationship between manga and anime.

For supporting the realization of this complex project, I would like to extend special thanks to: Michiko Yamakawa, archivist at Production I.G, who was an invaluable source throughout this undertaking – she not only provided many of the illustrations but also gave helpful advice on the final selection, and I felt very honoured to work with her in the studio's archive; Yukie Saeki at Studio 4°C for her kind cooperation in the provision of work by Shinji Kimura; Kumi Shimizu at Kodansha for her patience and dedication to getting the material from *AKIRA* and *Ghost in the Shell* ready for publication – my apologies for all the back and forth before finally arriving at the final selection and agreement; Véronique Millet at Bandai Namco Arts Inc. for her cooperation in clearing the rights for *Metropolis*; Shigekazu Fujisawa at Genco for his very cooperative and friendly response to our request to publish the Patlabor materials; Rie Shimasue and Ikki Todoroki at Studio Khara for their professional and in every way superlative assistance in publishing the work of Hideaki Anno; Asako Iwabuchi at Mori Building Co. Ltd for her very helpful insights and assistance in locating long sought-after material; David d'Heilly and his wife Shizu Yuasa for their continued support and hospitality, which helped to nurture this project from its earliest phases; and Haruka Saito for her continued interest and support of my work, as well as housing me during several visits to Tokyo.

I also thank the rights holders for generously granting the rights to publish the images: Aniplex, Bandai Namco Arts Inc., Genco, Kajima, Kodansha Co. Ltd., Mori Building Co. Ltd, Ogura Koubo, Production I.G, Studio 4°C and Studio Khara.

I would also like to thank Darren Wall for bringing up the idea for this publication and for reaching out to me. My deep gratitude goes to Lucas Dietrich and the team at Thames & Hudson, especially Evie Tarr, for their continued trust and confidence in the realization of this beautiful publication. I thank John Jervis for his insightful corrections and remarks during the editing process, which helped to bring out what the author really wanted to say.

I wholeheartedly thank Julia Glaß for accompanying me through this project from its conception, and for coming up with the simplest and best title for the end result.

The research for this publication was funded and supported by Les Jardins des Pilotes e.V. für Kunst und Kultur, Berlin. I thank our chairman Andreas Broeckmann for his continued and generous support of the undertaking.

And finally I would like to extend my deepest gratitude to Hiroko Myokam for her tireless efforts and her wise insights, through which she has assisted in this undertaking from the very beginning. Without your help this journey would not have ended so successfully.

About movie titles and artists' names
Japanese and overseas studios that release anime into English-language markets do not always follow the same romanization rules, therefore there is a certain level of confusion regarding the spelling of both movie titles and artists' names. For the purpose of this publication, I have chosen to follow the most common versions. This approach is inspired by Jonathan Clements and Helen McCarthy, and should help the reader to access more information on specific titles in their *Anime Encyclopedia* (2015). For reference purposes, the kanji of the artists' names are given in the biography section.

AKIRA, cut no. 1
Still images

AKIRA

With its multi-layered cityscapes, Katsuhiro Otomo's *AKIRA* was a milestone in the global popularity of anime, presenting an exuberant vision of a future megacity, and converting a generation of illustrators to the joys of abandoned buildings, dusty corners and decaying backyards.

AKIRA, 1988. **DIR.:** Katsuhiro Otomo. **SCR.:** Katsuhiro Otomo, Izo Hashimoto. **ART:** Toshiharu Mizutani. **ANI.:** Takashi Nakamura. **MUS.:** Geinoh Yamashirogumi. **PRD.:** AKIRA Committee. 124 mins. Based on the graphic novel AKIRA by Katsuhiro Otomo first published by Young Magazine, Kodansha Ltd.

AKIRA, cut no. 1
Final production background, *detail*
Toshiharu Mizutani
Poster colour on paper
93 × 53 cm (36⅝ × 20⅞ in.)

Tokyo on 16 July 1988, the first cut of *AKIRA*. The high-rise buildings in the centre are part of Shinjuku. The camera pans up from the bottom of the artwork. A bomb explodes around Mitaka City, just behind Shinjuku. The blast erases the cityscape.

Although this is the first cut of the film, the background was drawn as the last piece of the production by art director Toshiharu Mizutani. Takashi Watabe, one of the most prolific concept and layout designers featured in this volume, prepared the layout. Usually the layout drawing would be transferred to the background paper but, because time was running out, Mizutani painted directly on the layout. It took him two and a half days to finish this oversized piece (Mizutani, personal interview, 3 June 2019).

In 1988, a massive explosion destroys Tokyo and ignites the Third World War. By the year 2019, Tokyo has been rebuilt, and is now known as Neo Tokyo. The city prepares to host the Olympics the following year but is plagued by terrorism. Two youngsters, Tetsuo and Kaneda, are out racing with their friends against a rival motorcycle gang. Tetsuo crashes his bike into a child with the face of an old man, and is then swiftly taken away by the military.

The accident awakens psychic powers in Tetsuo. Gradually he comes to understand that he is just one of several experimental subjects of a secret government programme to replicate Akira, the singularity that caused the explosion in 1988. Tetsuo learns that he can gain help from Akira, who is located in cryogenic storage beneath the Olympic Stadium's construction site, and so he escapes from hospital. At the stadium, losing control of his powers, Tetsuo mutates into a gigantic mass that consumes all matter, including his friend Kaneda.

As this mass grows, the child with the aged face and his siblings awaken Akira in order to try to stop it. Akira then creates a bright, sphere-shaped force field, reminiscent of the halo effect produced by an exploding bomb, which draws Tetsuo and Kaneda into another dimension. In addition, the sphere created by Akira also destroys Neo Tokyo, echoing Tokyo's earlier destruction. While floating weightless, Kaneda experiences Tetsuo's childhood, including Tetsuo's dependence on Kaneda during their youth, and how the two of them were trained and altered before Tokyo's destruction. The sphere then disappears and water floods the city. Tetsuo vanishes into his own universe. Kaneda and his friends have survived, and they drive off into the ruins of the city.

Katsuhiro Otomo adapted the film's plot from his own manga, which ran in Kodansha's *Young Magazine* from 1982 to 1990. The film was almost solely responsible for the boom in anime among English-speaking viewers during the early 1990s. For many among this new audience, *AKIRA* was the first film that they perceived as anime – as specifically Japanese animation. As such, it had a tremendous influence on a whole generation of film enthusiasts.

AKIRA is a visual tour de force. At the time of production, it was the most expensive anime ever made. Apart from the ingenious artwork, both the dynamic approach to editing and the extremely fluid motion were unlike anything seen before. Much of AKIRA's cinematic power stems from the opulent representation of Neo Tokyo itself, and the lavish spectacle of its final destruction. The towering high-rise buildings that appear in the background of many of the low-angle cuts are obviously inspired by the urban design of Fritz Lang's Metropolis (1927).

The influence of Ridley Scott's Blade Runner (1982) on AKIRA is undeniable, resonating strongly throughout the project. The anime is even set in the same year as the seminal cyberpunk film. Furthermore, parts of its cityscape seem to be direct extensions of Blade Runner's set. Another major influence on the design of Neo Tokyo was the work of architect Kenzo Tange. His design for the Yoyogi National Gymnasium in Tokyo, completed in 1964, acted as the blueprint for Neo Tokyo's Olympic Stadium. And, most importantly, the idea of locating Neo Tokyo on a landfill in Tokyo Bay was drawn directly from Tange's radical urban scheme A Plan for Tokyo, 1960: Toward a Structural Reorganization (1961).

Otomo has stated that he conceived the film more as a visual work than an animated story with characters, thus he put a strong emphasis on the film's production design (Otomo 1989). The action takes place mainly at night, and a look at the colour chart reveals a tremendous variety of dark hues, many of which would not usually appear in animation. Kimie Yamana, the production's chief colourist, noted that 'there's such subtlety in the variations that you wouldn't notice them on a television screen, but in the theatre it really makes a difference' (Otomo 1989). This is one of the primary reasons for the outstanding quality of the film's artwork. Much of the production took place at the AKIRA Production Studio in Mitaka – seventy staff members were employed to do the artwork, while 327 individual colours were used to achieve the desired effects (Otomo 1989).

Many of the final production backgrounds feature rather unusual formats due to the extraordinary camerawork. As the action in AKIRA is very dynamic, the camera is required to be similarly dynamic, often following the characters by panning past a large background illustration.

AKIRA
Image board, pre-production
Toshiharu Mizutani
Poster colour on paper
25 × 35 cm (9⅞ × 13⅞ in.)

Before appointing Toshiharu Mizutani as art director for AKIRA, its director Katsuhiro Otomo also considered Nizo Yamamoto for the role. In the pre-production phase, Otomo asked both to deliver sample images of their work in order to decide on the ideal candidate. He briefed both artists with his initial ideas for the look of the feature – this and the following image board were produced by Mizutani and Yamamoto respectively during this casting process.

AKIRA
Image board, pre-production
Nizo Yamamoto
Poster colour on paper
40 × 29 cm (15¾ × 11½ in.)

Nizo Yamamoto, born in 1953, is a well-known anime art director and background artist. He is famous for his work on several of the Studio Ghibli films directed by Hayao Miyazaki and Isao Takahata, including *Laputa: Castle in the Sky* (1986), *Grave of the Fireflies* (1988), *Only Yesterday* (1991), *Whisper of the Heart* (1995), *Princess Mononoke* (1997) and *Spirited Away* (2001). Yamamoto left Studio Ghibli after the completion of *Spirited Away* and now works at his own company, Kaieisha.

AKIRA, cut no. 259
Still image

Army helicopters fly over Neo Tokyo towards the old town.

AKIRA, cut no. 259
Image board
Toshiharu Mizutani
Poster colour on paper
26 × 37 cm (10¼ × 14⅝ in.)

To emphasize the vastness of Neo Tokyo, Otomo staged his scenes in several locations spread across the entire city. The government research labs, the run-down bars and the construction zone of the stadium act as isolated spaces, linked by highways and flyovers (Otomo 1989).

The annotations on this image board by Mizutani include one telling the art team to increase the lighting in the streets a little (comment on the left side). The arrow at the top right corner points to the old town, which is suffering a power cut, thus retains its dark hues. Around the bay area, however, small lights were later added.

AKIRA, cut no. 417
Image board
Toshiharu Mizutani
Poster colour on paper
26 × 37 cm (10¼ × 14⅝ in.)

Neo Tokyo is depicted at night in this image board by Mizutani showing the view from the colonel's helicopter as he flies to the Olympic Stadium's construction site (see opposite). There are a lot of night scenes in *AKIRA*, and these usually employ blue hues to create the desired dim effect. However, Mizutani made occasional use of an alternative, unorthodox colour scheme stressing reds and greens. This was an experiment he had always wanted to try, and Otomo gave it his backing (Otomo 1989).

AKIRA, cut no. 417
Still image

AKIRA, cut no. 334
Image board
Toshiharu Mizutani
Poster colour on paper
26 × 37 cm (10¼ × 14⅝ in.)

This image board depicts the road leading to the site of the explosion that had destroyed Tokyo in 1988. In the final production background, the lettering on the advertisement was altered.

AKIRA, cut no. 334
Still image

AKIRA, cut no. unspecified
Image board
Toshiharu Mizutani
Poster colour on paper
26 × 37 cm (10¼ × 14⅝ in.)

Mizutani used a more conventional colour scheme for this dawn scene. The location is a water channel, similar to that in cut no. 1489 (see p. 43). The annotations on the right-hand side specify that 'the windows reflect the bright sky' and 'only the sky is bright', while those next to the arrow on the left indicate that the 'purple colour should not be more intense than the hue on the left side of the cityscape'.

AKIRA, cut no. 126
Still images

AKIRA, cut no. 126
Image board
Hiroshi Ono
Poster colour on paper
23 × 32 cm (9⅛ × 12⅝ in.)

Arcades and a wide road frame a vibrant shopping street. The initial image board was warped in the layout process to accommodate a pan shot following a fast-moving motorcycle. The comment below the illustration specifies that the lighting of the street should be green.

AKIRA, cut no. 543
Image board
Toshiharu Mizutani
Poster colour on paper
26 × 37 cm (10¼ × 14⅝ in.)

An image board of the vocational training school that Kaneda and his friends attend. This view does not appear in the film – in the end, the shot was taken from another angle, although the same architectural design was used.

AKIRA, cut no. 84
Final production background
Toshiharu Mizutani
Poster colour on paper
42 × 39 cm (16⅝ × 15⅜ in.)

An alley behind Harukiya, a bar located in the east of the city that has become a gathering place for the protagonists' friends (Otomo 2002, p. 154). This large production background was used for a pan down from the illuminated skyline into the shady back street.

AKIRA, cut no. 84
Still image

AKIRA, cut no. 134
Final production background
Artist unknown
Poster colour on paper
24 × 57 cm (9½ × 22½ in.)

Bird's-eye view into a back alley behind the shopping arcade depicted in cut no. 126 (see p. 27).

AKIRA, cut no. 134
Still image

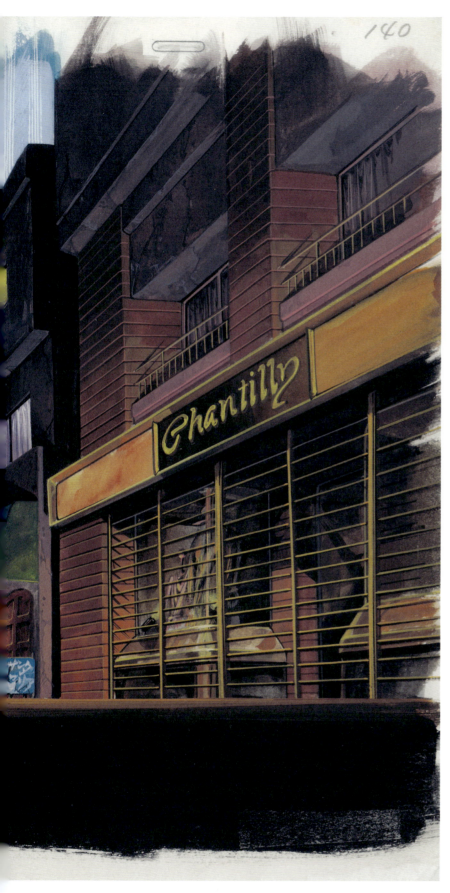

AKIRA, cut no. 140
Final production background
Toshiharu Mizutani
Poster colour on paper
25.5 × 36 cm (10⅛ × 14¼ in.)

This shot from a low angle emphasizes *AKIRA*'s dystopian vision of the future. Superficially, the city seems to be glamorous, yet the streets lie littered with garbage and the walls are sprayed with graffiti. The contrast between the colours of the street and those of the high-rise buildings enforces the impression of the complex layering of Neo Tokyo's social and physical structures.

AKIRA, cut no. 140
Still image

AKIRA, cut no. 180
Final production background
Toshiharu Mizutani
Poster colour on paper
25.5 × 36 cm (10⅛ × 14¼ in.)

Searchlights scour the sky in a scene reminiscent of Fritz Lang's *Metropolis* (1927).

AKIRA, cut no. 180
Still image

34   AKIRA

AKIRA, cut no. 700
Final production background
Toshiharu Mizutani
Poster colour on paper
26 × 37 cm (10¼ × 14⅝ in.)

Another night view of Neo Tokyo, with green and red focal points that contrast with the overall blue hues, creating an extraordinarily atmospheric urban environment.

AKIRA, cut no. 700
Still image

AKIRA, cut no. 214
Final production background
Toshiharu Mizutani
Poster colour on paper
25.5 × 37 cm (10⅛ × 14⅝ in.)

The city is rocked by terrorist attacks and the military steps up its presence on the streets. Society seems to be teetering on the brink of collapse.

AKIRA, cut no. 214
Still image

AKIRA, cut no. 210
Final production background
Toshiharu Mizutani
Book, two layers superimposed,
poster colour on paper and cel
25.5 × 36 cm (10⅛ × 14¼ in.)

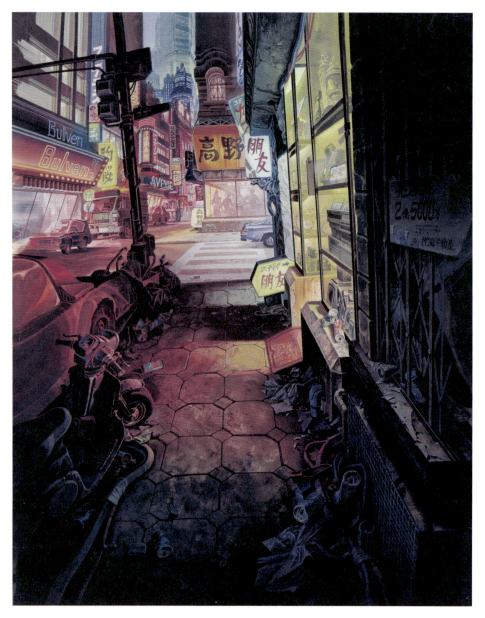

AKIRA, cut no. 182
Final production background
Toshiharu Mizutani
Poster colour on paper
55 × 43 cm (21¾ × 17 in.)

A back alley with pubs, snacks and ramen shops. This production background is used to depict the first-person perspective of a wounded man staggering down the street. He has been hit by a bullet and is suffering from loss of blood, thus his vision is blurred as he tries to comprehend the environment. The blur effect was created by using multiple exposures during the photographic process. The camera moves quickly across the large tableau.

AKIRA, cut no. 182
Still images

AKIRA, cut no. 207
Final production background
Toshiharu Mizutani
Poster colour on paper
42 × 36 cm (16⅝ × 14¼ in.)

Neo Tokyo is built on a landfill in Tokyo Bay, therefore space is limited, with the city growing upwards rather than expanding horizontally. Bridges, elevators and high viewpoints, as in this cut, are important to achieve the impression of a deeply structured, multi-layered cityscape.

AKIRA, cut no. 207
Still image

In the streets of Neo Tokyo, demonstrators and police clash.

AKIRA, cut no. 1542
Final production background, book
Artist unknown
Two layers superimposed, poster colour on paper and cel
26 × 40 cm (10¼ × 15¾ in.)

Downtown Neo Tokyo as its final destruction draws near. As the story reaches its climax the main protagonist, Tetsuo, discovers his psychokinetic powers. In this scene, he attacks a helicopter, which then crashes into the building on the left.

AKIRA, cut no. 1542
Still image

AKIRA, cut no. 1544
Final production background, book
Artist unknown
Two layers superimposed, poster colour on paper and cel
26 × 40 cm (10¼ × 15¾ in.)

The destroyed wall is drawn on a cel and superimposed on the background.
Using this masking technique, debris is added to the side of the building.

AKIRA, cut no. 554
Final production background
Artist unknown
Poster colour on paper
25 × 47.7 cm (9⅞ × 18⅞ in.)

Cuts nos 554 and 1489 (opposite) are examples of Mizutani's attempts to break with conventional colour schemes for urban scenery in anime. Here, he uses an extreme palette of green and red instead to give Neo Tokyo an uncanny appearance.

AKIRA, cut no. 554
Still image

AKIRA, cut no. 1489
Final production background
Toshiharu Mizutani
Poster colour on paper
25.5 × 36 cm (10⅛ × 14¼ in.)

AKIRA, cut no. 2106
Image board
Toshiharu Mizutani
Poster colour on paper
15 × 33 cm (6 × 13 in.)

Driving on his motorcycle, Kaneda remembers his childhood. The intensity of the prevailing dark colour scheme is replaced by a hue in a higher key, and the city takes on a luminous appearance.

AKIRA, cut no. 2106
Still images

AKIRA, cuts nos 954, 955 and 956
Still image

The movement towards this high-rise building was created by blending three production backgrounds. Its countless windows give the impression that the structure is far larger than any building that existed in Tokyo at the time of the film's release.

AKIRA, cut no. 954
Image board
Toshiharu Mizutani
Poster colour on paper
16 × 30 cm (6⅜ × 11⅞ in.)

This image depicts one of the tallest buildings in the centre of Neo Tokyo, the high-security research centre that houses a laboratory for the army's military-research facility. The film's protagonist, Tetsuo, is detained in a hospital in the central part of the structure. The architecture and lighting of the scene are reminiscent of *Blade Runner*'s set design. In particular, the pyramid-like pod at the bottom of the high-rise resembles the headquarters of Tyrell Corporation, the android manufacturer in Ridley Scott's film (Mead, Hodgetts & Villeneuve 2017, p. 127). The camera's approach to the building was created by blending three production backgrounds one after the other. This image board was used as a blueprint for the first background (cut no. 954).

AKIRA, cut no. 1169
Final production background
Artist unknown
Poster colour on paper
35 × 116 cm (13⅞ × 45¾ in.)

This is the largest production background featured in this book. It depicts pipes in the central core of the research facility (see p. 45). The camera slides quickly over this backdrop from right to left to follow a flying vehicle.

AKIRA, cut no. 1176
Final production background
Artist unknown
Poster colour on paper
48 × 41 cm (19 × 16¼ in.)

This is the same central supply core as shown in cut no. 1169 opposite, seen from another angle. The shaft holds an organic assembly of various utilities such as electricity, water, gas and communication services.

AKIRA, cut no. 426
Final production background
Artist unknown
Poster colour on paper
39 × 40 cm (15⅜ × 15¾ in.)

The Olympic Stadium is an important location in *AKIRA*. Beneath the stadium's construction site, the remains of the supernatural Akira entity are stored in a cryogenic chamber.

AKIRA debuted as a manga in 1982, and the anime was released in 1988. In both, the narrative is set in the year 2019 and, for unknown reasons, Otomo envisaged that the Olympic Games would take place in Neo Tokyo the following year. In reality, Tokyo had hosted the Games once before, in 1964, and in 2013 it won the bidding process to host them again in 2020. The sign in this final production background reads: '147 Days Until the Tokyo Olympics'. Underneath, it reads, 'With everyone's effort, let's make this a success'.

AKIRA, cut no. 1986
Still image

AKIRA, cut no. 1986
Image board
Toshiharu Mizutani
Poster colour on paper
17 × 30 cm (6¾ × 11⅞ in.)

Inside the stadium, construction is still under way, but a section on the left has just been destroyed by the accident that leads up to the film's final showdown (see cut no. 1924, p. 50).

AKIRA, cut no. 1924
Image board
Toshiharu Mizutani
Poster colour on paper
17 × 30 cm (6¾ × 11⅞ in.)

A part of the stadium, which is still under construction, has just been destroyed.
In this final image, Kaori climbs the stairs from the bottom and then sees Tetsuo.

AKIRA, cut no. 1924
Still image

AKIRA, cut no. 2177
Still image

AKIRA, cut no. 2177
Image board
Toshiharu Mizutani
Poster colour on paper
17 × 30 cm (6¾ × 11⅞ in.)

Once the clouds clear over the grounds of the Olympic Stadium, a large crater is visible. The stadium has been destroyed in the final cataclysmic explosion. Neo Tokyo is devastated once more, and water floods the ruins of the city.

AKIRA, cut no. 2204
Image board
Toshiharu Mizutani
Poster colour on paper
25 × 36 cm (9⅞ × 14¼ in.)

Celestial light breaks through the clouds, possibly originating from Tetsuo's new location in space and time. The annotation on the right-hand side specifies that this light has not yet touched the rubbish in the foreground.

AKIRA, cut no. 2204
Still image

In the final image, the direction of the light was changed.

AKIRA, cut no. 2175
Final production background, book
Hiromasa Ogura
Two layers superimposed, poster colour on paper and cel
30 × 47 cm (11⅞ × 18⅝ in.)

In the final phase of production, time was running out so Mizutani mobilized his colleagues and asked for their assistance. Hiromasa Ogura came to help, producing this final production background. The painting technique, the level of abstraction in the buildings' textures and the overall look and feel are typical of his style (Mizutani, personal interview, 3 June 2019). Ogura is not credited in the film's end titles.

AKIRA, cut no. 2211
Image board
Toshiharu Mizutani
Poster colour on paper
29 × 21.5 cm (11½ × 8½ in.)

AKIRA, cut no. 2211
Still images

AKIRA, cut no. 2211
Final production background
Hiroshi Ono
Poster colour on paper
50 × 36 cm (19¾ × 14¼ in.)

After the final explosion, three friends of the deceased protagonist find themselves on the outskirts of Neo Tokyo. They drive off on their motorcycles into the ruins of the city.

In Japan's post-war economy, construction and reconstruction have often been placed centre stage. In this so-called 'construction state' (*doken kokka*), large amounts of public money have been used in numerous dam, highway and civic building projects. Whether such projects are necessary or in the public interest is highly questionable. As symbolized by the construction of the new Olympic Stadium and its subsequent destruction, *AKIRA* expresses the joy and sense of liberation that accompanies cataclysmic devastation, with its tearing down of old institutions. Otomo shares this counter-cultural idealism, which harks back to the 1960s, with his contemporary Mamoru Oshii.

PATLABOR: THE MOVIE

In Mamoru Oshii's early classic, Tokyo is re-imagined as it might be in the near future, and emerges as the film's main protagonist. Working with the finest talents in anime, Oshii perfected his technique of using background pictures to create spatial narratives.

Patlabor: The Movie, 1989. DIR.: Mamoru Oshii. SCR.: Kazunori Ito. ART: Hiromasa Ogura. ANI.: Kazuchika Kise, Koji Sawai. MUS.: Kenji Kawai. PRD: I.G Tatsunoko, Studio Deen. 118 mins.

Patlabor: The Movie,
cut no. 184
Final production background, *detail*
Hiromasa Ogura
Poster colour on paper
25 × 35.3 cm (9⅞ × 14 in.)

Two detectives cross under this bridge during their trip on a waterway. In the storyboard, the director Mamoru Oshii specified that this cut should present a 'dark space'. For his vision of the city, Oshii favoured backgrounds with strong contrasts between dark and light. However, art director Hiromasa Ogura preferred to take into consideration how certain details could be emphasized and others dropped in order to achieve a strong overall contrast, instead of taking one all-encompassing approach. In any case, for Oshii it was most important that the scenes depicting Tokyo's cityscape had 'quality, texture and substance'.

The film is set in Tokyo in the year 1999. At the close of the twentieth century, a rise in global sea levels forces a massive building programme in Tokyo – the Babylon Project – which reclaims more land from Tokyo Bay. The story centres on big robots piloted by humans and used mainly for construction work, the so-called 'Labors'. The police set up a 'Pat[rol] Labor division' to deal with the crime that this new technology brings.

For this production, director Mamoru Oshii assembled many of the leading talents working in modern anime, and developed his signature technique of crafting a spatial narrative through the background artwork. Through this means, the city of Tokyo acts as the film's protagonist. This is most apparent in a scene at the start of the second part of the film, in which two detectives walk around Tokyo tracing the footsteps of the villain. Oshii has explained his intentions as follows: 'The purpose of this scene is not to depict the characters, but to depict the city of Tokyo itself. In most movies, this would be the midpoint, when the plot can seem to get bogged down as it alters direction. But in this film, I consider this part to be its ultimate climax. The first opening shots in this scene do not even attempt to explain what's going on here. It's structured so that the scenery is brought out first, then after a few more shots, it becomes clear what's going on.' In such subsequent works as *Patlabor 2: The Movie* (1993) and *Ghost in the Shell* (1995), Oshii included similar scenes.

The film's detailed, carefully elaborated cityscapes, as well as its story set in a near future that was already beginning to loom on viewers' horizons, made it a hit with audiences and critics alike. Oshii's concept when creating a realistic setting was not to invent an entirely new cityscape for Tokyo ten years in the future, but instead to show the existing city as it might be in a decade's time. For the team around art director Hiromasa Ogura, this meant it was important to draw Tokyo as it was at the time of production in 1989, yet altered as if were 1999. Oshii's idea was 'to depict the face of Tokyo through action scenes without having the cityscape draw attention to itself'.

In achieving this vision, Oshii stated that the overriding theme for the film's cinematography had been 'how successfully the team could avoid the typical camera angles and framing used in ordinary animation'. As a result, unusual camera angles had to be found and the whole art team went on extensive location-hunting trips in the Tokyo Metropolitan Area, often exploiting unfamiliar perspectives from its waterways.

Patlabor: The Movie, cut no. 182
Final production background
Hiromasa Ogura
Poster colour on paper
18 × 25.5 cm (7⅛ × 10⅛ in.)

Patlabor: The Movie marked the first time that realistic background paintings had been placed at the forefront of the action. This final production background presents a panoramic view of the Kanda River near the Hijiri Bridge in Tokyo's Ochanomizu area. The bridge is a Tokyo landmark, and inspired other structures such as the Otonashi Bridge in Takinogawa, Kita City. Although many people know the location, this perspective from the waterway is unusual, and can only be seen from a boat.

Patlabor: The Movie, cut no. 186
Final production background
Hiromasa Ogura
Poster colour on paper
25 × 35.3 cm (9⅞ × 14 in.)

The two detectives' journey on the waterway ends here and they disembark in front of the wooden structure, a floating apartment building. To achieve a realistic depiction of the old town, Ogura developed high-contrast images that reflect the quality of the light in a Tokyo summer. A wide range of shades of green gives the scene a slightly melancholy atmosphere.

Patlabor: The Movie, location photography
Haruhiko Higami
Black-and-white photography, small-format negative print

The story of *Patlabor: The Movie* takes place in Tokyo in the year 1999. The film gives a relatively realistic and critical picture of the structural changes already taking place in Tokyo's cityscape. Location photographer Haruhiko Higami and the art team embarked on a journey through the city to discover new and unfamiliar views. Higami's photographs were taken in black-and-white to avoid hampering the art director's choice of colour palette.

Patlabor: The Movie, cut no. 279
Final production background
Shuichi Kusamori
Poster colour on paper
25 × 35.3 cm (9⅞ × 14 in.)

A bird cage hangs from the second-floor window. Usually, the background painting in anime productions is seen as a minor issue – greater importance is given to the characters that move in front of these backgrounds. However, in several sequences in *Patlabor: The Movie* the background art comes to the fore and actually emerges as the narrator of the story. As Mamoru Oshii explains, camera movement in this scene, which lasts approximately five minutes (cuts nos 270–312), is exceptionally slow in order to 'give a sense of weight to the background'.

Patlabor: The Movie, cut no. 423
Final production background
Shuichi Kusamori
Poster colour on paper
38 × 34 cm (15 × 13½ in.)

This large production background was created to allow for a panning shot from the bottom to the top.

Patlabor: The Movie, cut no. 423
Still images

Patlabor: The Movie, cut no. 281
Final production background
Hiromasa Ogura
Poster colour on paper
25 × 35.3 cm (9⅞ × 14 in.)

The site of a demolished apartment –
a striking outline of the building that once
stood on the site is visible on the wall.

Patlabor: The Movie, location photography
Haruhiko Higami
Black-and-white photography, small-format negative print

Patlabor: The Movie, cut no. 281
Still image

Patlabor: The Movie, cut no. 308
Still image

Patlabor: The Movie, cut no. 308
Final production background
Hiromasa Ogura
Poster colour on paper
25 × 35.3 cm (9⅞ × 14 in.)

In this striking image, a 'Labor' robot is dismantling the apartment building in the centre. The detective sits on a tiled remnant from a demolished building watching the bleak scene.

Patlabor: The Movie, cut no. 310
Still image

Patlabor: The Movie, cut no. 310
Final production background
Hiromasa Ogura
Poster colour on paper
25 × 35.3 cm (9⅞ × 14 in.)

Unlike many European cities, where old buildings are frequently refurbished and given new life, entire neighbourhoods in Tokyo are often demolished and rebuilt. Houses are abandoned, leaving only traces of their inhabitants, and in time they gradually disappear, to be replaced by new buildings.

Patlabor: The Movie, cut no. 382
Final production background
Hiromasa Ogura
Poster colour on paper
25 × 35.3 cm (9⅞ × 14 in.)

Oshii specified this cut in the storyboard as 'a vacant lot surrounded by a fence. We can see that it was once an orderly and well-maintained block, but now not even a single blade of grass is growing there. An abandoned building with overwhelming presence. An almost fictitious-looking new building behind. The entire scene shimmers in the heat.' The atmospheric character of the old house is evoked by placing it at the focal point of the perspective, and by rendering it with fine lines in great detail, in contrast to the rather flat and sketchy depiction of the high-rise structures in the background.

Patlabor: The Movie, cut no. 382
Still image

PATLABOR 2: THE MOVIE

To achieve its intense, realistic depiction of Tokyo as an inner-city warzone, unprecedented efforts were put into the layouts for *Patlabor 2*. The film's complex themes and innovative creative approach were to have a profound influence on the entire anime industry.

Patlabor 2: The Movie, 1993. DIR.: Mamoru Oshii. SCR.: Kazunori Ito. ART: Hiromasa Ogura. ANI.: Kazuchika Kise. MUS.: Kenji Kawai. PRD.: Production I.G. 113 mins.

The story is set in the winter of 2002, three years after the events of the first movie. Out of the blue, the Yokohama Bay Bridge is bombed by a missile. A video taken by chance at the scene shows what seems to be an F-16 fighter in the vicinity – it appears that the jet may be one operated by the Japan Air Self-Defense Force (JASDF). The Japan Ground Self-Defense Force (JGSDF), another arm of Japan's armed forces, respond to this rumour with a military takeover of Tokyo and the imposition of martial law. Public panic rises as JGSDF-marked helicopters attack several bridges in Tokyo Bay and destroy various communication centres. In addition, Special Assault Team snipers shoot down an auto-piloted blimp that has been responsible for jamming all electronics in the Greater Tokyo Area. When the blimp crashes in the dense city centre, it releases a seemingly deadly gas. The former members of the original Patlabor team reunite one last time in order to stop the madness, having concluded that the current police command can no longer bring the situation under control.

When Mamoru Oshii is introduced abroad, his later project *Ghost in the Shell* (1995) is usually the focus of attention due to its international fame. However, Oshii himself ranks *Patlabor 2: The Movie* as his most important work because of its intense exploration of Japan as a country and a society (Oshii 1993b, p. 142). Released in theatres in 1993, it proved to be a milestone for both its director and Japanese animation. It was the first work in which Oshii brought animation and a story involving real social phenomena together on the same screen. After almost fifty years without war, Japan had become totally habituated to peace. However, not long after the movie's release, the nation was rudely awakened to its fragility by two major disasters: the Kobe earthquake and a terrorism incident on Tokyo's subway involving a religious cult, both of which occurred in 1995. The fact that scenes from these two disasters had been foreshadowed in *Patlabor 2* led to an even greater appreciation for the film.

Patlabor 2 was created by Production I.G, the same studio that had worked on the first Patlabor film. The commitment to the project shown by I.G was instrumental in realizing this difficult film with its complex themes. The narratives created by Oshii tend to lose authenticity and gravity in the absence of well-grounded and convincing visuals – devoid of good animation, his works cannot attain their full potential. The high quality

Patlabor 2: The Movie,
cut no. 201
Final production background,
detail
Hiromasa Ogura
Poster colour on paper
25.5 × 36 cm (10⅛ × 14¼ in.)

This production background shows the Yokohama Bay Bridge. The illustration is used as a secondary diegetic image in a TV advertisement just before the bridge is bombed by a missile, igniting the story. In *Patlabor 2*, Oshii makes frequent use of this 'image within an image' technique.

of Production I.G's work ensured that this requirement was met on *Patlabor 2*, and the project contributed significantly to the direction that Production I.G itself was to take in the future. The studio became a sponsoring partner in the production of *Patlabor 2*, and its financial investment and drive for artistic quality continued in such films by Oshii as *Ghost in the Shell* and *Innocence* (2004), ensuring new standards in animation were achieved in all of these major projects.

The overall tone of *Patlabor 2* is dark and sombre. Most of the shots are executed from a fixed camera perspective, and tracking shots are done at an even pace. The subdued tone and gradual pacing allow the viewer to meander through the film's metaphors and its imagery of water, fish, dogs and birds – all the distinctive iconography that forms such a strong feature of Oshii's style. Films that possess qualities that a mature public can appreciate are a rarity in anime, thus *Patlabor 2* was embraced by older audiences who had often been left dissatisfied by previous anime.

In this production, Oshii put an unprecedented focus on and effort into the layout stage. Five highly skilled artists were entrusted with the task of developing layouts: Takashi Watabe, Satoshi Kon, Atsushi Takeuchi, Yoshio Mizumura and Masatsugu Arakawa. Watabe and Takeuchi have since become frequent collaborators with Oshii, while Kon became an anime director himself. The layout stage was allotted twice as much time in the production schedule as the animation itself (the creation of key animation and inbetween animation), making it clear where the primary creative work lay. This production method had a profound influence on the anime industry as a whole (Oshii 1993b, p. 16).

Patlabor 2: The Movie, location photography
Haruhiko Higami
Black-and-white photography, small-format negative print

This concept photo by Haruhiko Higami was taken prior to the film's production. For Oshii, 'the world obtained through the viewfinder is very different from that of the naked eye. The human eye, which has been detached from the city so much that it doesn't even realize that water is usually flowing in the rivers and moats, enters the city again through the viewfinder' (Oshii 1994, p. 33).

Patlabor 2: The Movie, cut no. 572
Final production background
Hiromasa Ogura
Poster colour on paper
29 × 38.7 cm (11½ × 15¼ in.)

An imaginary view of Sumida River from the north-east, suggesting how it might appear in 2002. The location looks similar today, although many more high-rise buildings have been built. In the background of the picture, the Tsukuda Bridge has already been the first target of a helicopter attack, and smoke rises from its ruins. From back to front the other bridges, attacked one after the other, are Chuo Bridge (suspension bridge), Eitai Bridge (semicircular structure) and Sumidagawa Bridge (in the foreground).

Patlabor 2: The Movie, cut no. 572
Still images

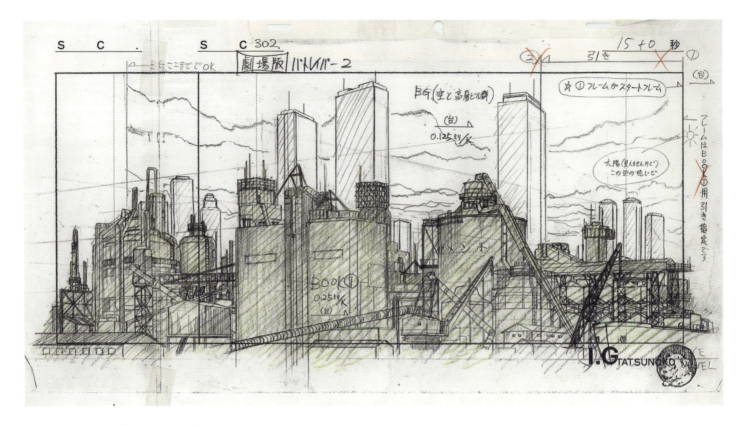

Patlabor 2: The Movie, cut no. 302
Layout
Hiromasa Ogura
Pencil on paper
26 × 44.8 cm (10¼ × 17¾ in.)

Art director Hiromasa Ogura drew these layouts for a meditative scene set in Tokyo Bay. This scene corresponds with similar scenes in *Patlabor: The Movie* (cuts nos 270–312), *Ghost in the Shell* (cuts nos 314–46) and *Innocence* (scene 36, cuts nos 1–45).

    The layout's foreground is based on a location-hunting photograph, but the background depicts high-rise buildings that do not in fact exist. The composition thus contrasts reality and fiction. Oshii's primary approach since *Patlabor: The Movie* has been 'a past full of presence and a future like a mirage' (Oshii 1994, p. 50). The movement of this shot – a long horizontal pan of the camera – is very slow, lasting fifteen seconds. This kind of shot puts a heavy burden on the quality of the photography, as it needs to be very precise to avoid jitter in the image.

Patlabor 2: The Movie, cut no. 302
Still image

Patlabor 2: The Movie, cut no. 311
Still images

Patlabor 2: The Movie, cut no. 311
Layout
Hiromasa Ogura
Pencil on paper
30.4 × 87.5 cm (12 × 34½ in.)

This extended cut is eighteen seconds long, and presents an abandoned factory – 'the mecca of action movies' – facing a waterway near Haneda Airport. The layout is based on a location-hunting photograph. Oshii comments that 'it is important to have a good eye for photography, including lens selection, when location hunting. If you are not technically confident, you need to employ a reliable photographer such as Haruhiko Higami. Be sure to shoot in black-and-white so as not to be swayed by the impression of the colours' (Oshii 1994, p. 51).

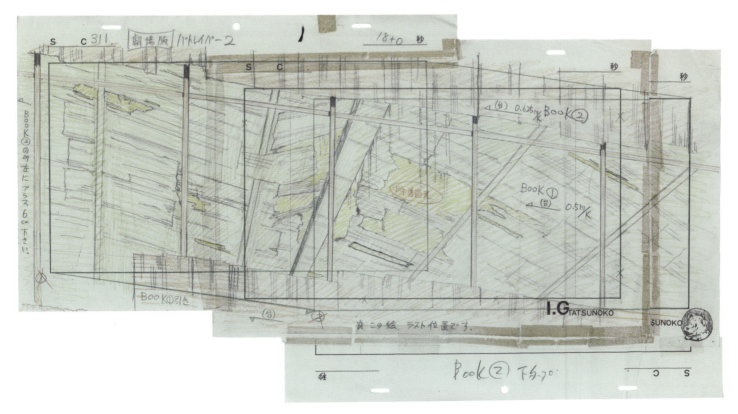

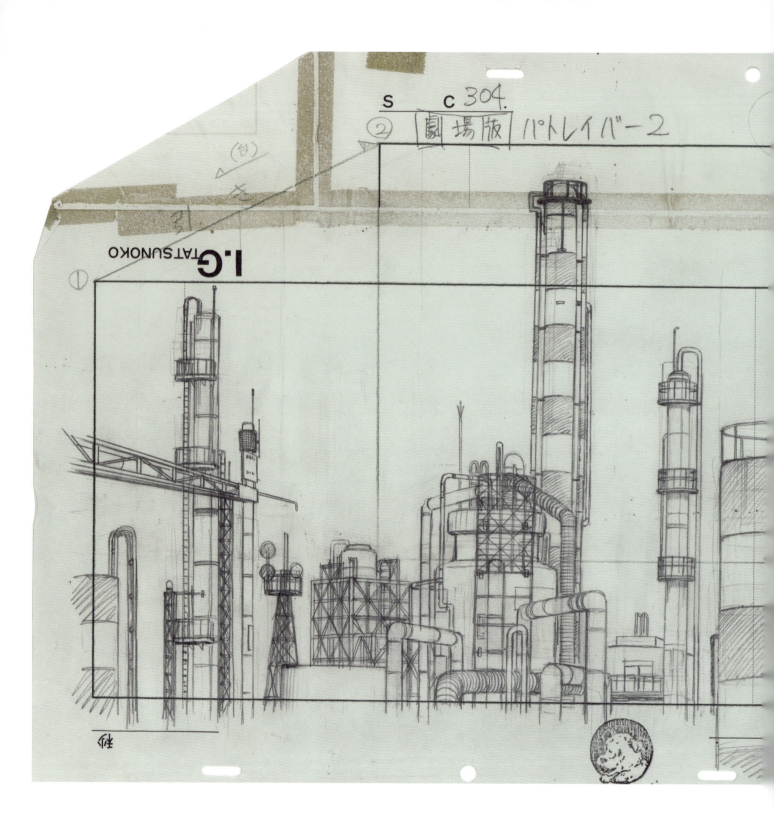

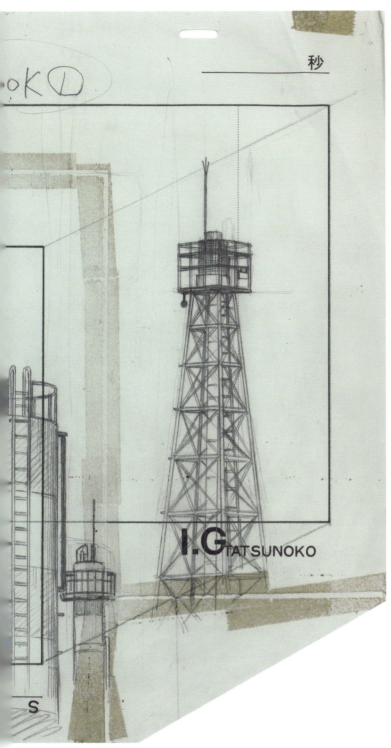

Patlabor 2: The Movie, cut no. 304
Layout
Hiromasa Ogura
Pencil on paper
29 × 47.5 cm (11½ × 18¾ in.)

While the scenery of the Tokyo Bay Area is being slowly surveyed in this long, twenty-five-second cut, the protagonist indulges in a typical Oshii-like monologue about peace and the coming war. Captain Goto tells his colleague: 'We're both officers, serving our country. What exactly are we trying to protect? Japan hasn't seen warfare since the Second World War. You and I have lived our entire lives in a time of peace. Peace – that's what we're fighting to protect. But what does peace really mean to Japan? [...] As war is followed by peace, peace inevitably leads to war. Someday we'll realize that peace is more than an absence of war. Have you considered that?'

Patlabor 2: The Movie, cut no. 304
Still images

Patlabor 2: The Movie, cut no. 354
Final production background, book
Hiromasa Ogura
Seven layers superimposed, poster colour on paper and cel
25.5 × 36 cm (10⅛ × 14¼ in.)

This production background is based on an elaborate layout by Satoshi Kon. It depicts a video screen in front of the Shinjuku Alta shopping centre. The layout is complex because the moving crowd at the back of the screen is reflected on the ceiling. As anime characters are line drawings, it is challenging to convey a feeling of enlargement or reduction. For Oshii, the representation of a secondary image on the video screen is an essential device to increase the realism of the cut. Kon was an expert in the creation of such self-referential imagery, and his later works such as *Paprika* (2006) rely thematically on the question of the screen's reality.

    This reproduction of the final production background is quite dark and the colours appear to be subdued because the layers have been stacked physically and then scanned.

Patlabor 2: The Movie, cut no. 416
Final production background, book
Hiromasa Ogura
Three layers superimposed, poster colour on paper and cel
25.5 × 36 cm (10⅛ × 14¼ in.)

This cut is based on a layout by Kon. The eye level is high above the street in order to contrast the people who will appear in the window on the right with the view into the distance. In order to emphasize this impression, these characters were also animated. Introducing this kind of character animation as part of the background is challenging to achieve in anime production because it disrupts the workflow of the key animator, who does not usually work directly with the art department (Oshii 1994, p. 62).

Patlabor 2: The Movie, cut no. 567
Final production background, book
Hiromasa Ogura
Two layers superimposed, poster colour on paper
25.5 × 36 cm (10⅛ × 14¼ in.)

This cut presents the Tsukuda Bridge (see the background of cut no. 572 on p. 72) being targeted during the helicopter attack. Compared to the first Patlabor film, the sequel employs completely different colour tones. *Patlabor 2* is basically monotone – a grey world. The production backgrounds of the attack scene are especially sombre.

Patlabor 2: The Movie, cut no. 567
Still images

80 Patlabor 2: The Movie

Patlabor 2: The Movie, cut no. 579
Still images

Patlabor 2: The Movie, cut no. 579
Final production background, book
Hiromasa Ogura
Two layers superimposed, poster colour
on paper and cel
25.5 × 36 cm (10⅛ × 14¼ in.)

The helicopters attack telecommunication systems with the aim of destroying a key part of the city's infrastructure.

Patlabor 2: The Movie, location photography
Haruhiko Higami
Black-and-white photography, small-format negative print

Location-hunting photography of Nihonbashi (literally 'Japan Bridge'). This picture was used for the last cut of the helicopter-attack scene, during which this important symbol of Tokyo is destroyed by a missile.

Nihonbashi gives its name to a commercial district in Tokyo, and is the point from which distances to other locations in the country are measured – the highway signs that indicate distances to the capital actually state the number of kilometres to Nihonbashi. Shortly before the 1964 Olympic Games, an expressway was built over the bridge, obscuring the classic view of Mount Fuji from its centre.

Patlabor 2: The Movie, cut no. 583
Still images

83

Patlabor 2: The Movie, cut no. 589
Final production background
Hiromasa Ogura
Poster colour on paper
25.5 × 36 cm (10⅛ × 14¼ in.)

A seemingly peaceful street in snowy Tokyo is disrupted by an explosion.

Patlabor 2: The Movie, cut no. 589
Still images

84   Patlabor 2: The Movie

Patlabor 2: The Movie, cut no. 617
Still image

Patlabor 2: The Movie, cut no. 617
Final production background
Hiromasa Ogura
Poster colour on paper
25.5 × 36 cm (10⅛ × 14¼ in.)

Viewed from the sky, the city appears to be far more vulnerable than New Port City, the fictional city that features in Oshii's later work *Ghost in the Shell* (1995).

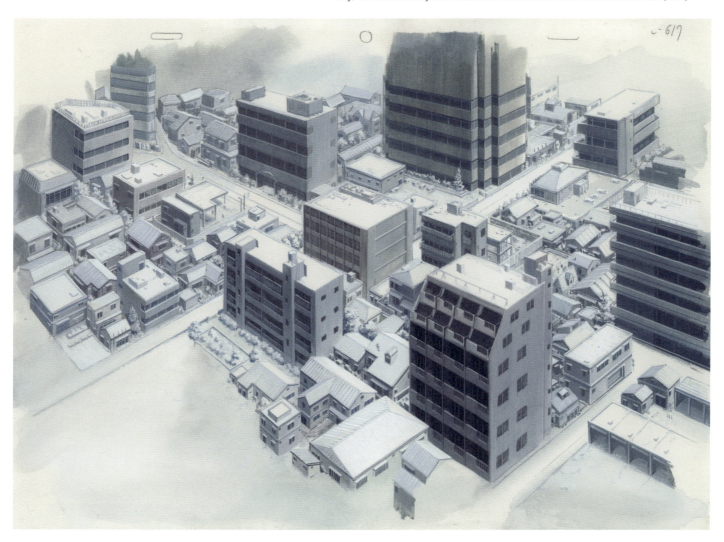

Patlabor 2: The Movie, cut no. 630
Final production background
Hiromasa Ogura
Poster colour on paper
25.5 × 36 cm (10⅛ × 14¼ in.)

This illustration shows the *tokonoma* (reception space) in the traditional Japanese house belonging to Nagumo, one of the main protagonists. The police officer rests in front of the alcove to meditate about her role in the final battle, which starts a few moments after this shot. The layout was prepared by Satoshi Kon.

Patlabor 2: The Movie, cut no. 632
Final production background
Hiromasa Ogura
Poster colour on paper
25.5 × 36 cm (10⅛ × 14¼ in.)

The view from Nagumo's living room into the garden. The layout for the shot was created by Kon, and the final image shows Nagumo sitting in front of the window looking out while a dog appears outside. *Patlabor 2* was the first film in which Oshii employed a basset, which would become a trademark, featuring in every subsequent production.

Patlabor 2: The Movie, cut no. 632
Still image

Patlabor 2: The Movie, cut no. 674
Final production background
Hiromasa Ogura
Poster colour on paper
25.5 × 36 cm (10⅛ × 14¼ in.)

This composition, based on a layout by Atsushi Takeuchi, captures the contrast between the width of Yasukuni Street (Tokyo Metropolitan Route 302) and the dimensions of the airship as it falls. The buildings on both sides have been tucked down slightly when compared to the actual location in Tokyo.

Patlabor 2: The Movie, cut no. 680
Still image

The shot-down blimp releases a gas in the city centre.

Patlabor 2: The Movie, cut no. 680
Final production background
Hiromasa Ogura
Poster colour on paper
25.5 × 36 cm (10⅛ × 14¼ in.)

To create images such as this, the art team went location-hunting by helicopter. 'There is nothing better than the real thing,' as director Mamoru Oshii has said (Oshii 1994, p. 67). By placing the point of view in the sky, height and breadth are emphasized while an impression of objectivity is produced.

Patlabor 2: The Movie, cut no. 685
Final production background
Hiromasa Ogura
Poster colour on paper
25.5 × 36 cm (10⅛ × 14¼ in.)

This shot presents a scene in front of Shinjuku's My City shopping centre. The eye level is kept below the frame.

Patlabor 2: The Movie, cut no. 685
Still image

Patlabor 2: The Movie, cut no. 728
Final production background
Hiromasa Ogura
Poster colour on paper
25.5 × 36 cm (10⅛ × 14¼ in.)

This background presents Shimbashi Subway Station on the Ginza Line. In the final battle, the Patlabor team uses an old stretch of this line to approach an artificial island, which the villain is employing as his hideout.

GHOST IN THE SHELL

Situated in a dark, dystopian cityscape that lies at the intersection of the traditional and the high-tech, *Ghost in the Shell* is a milestone in science fiction that draws on the urban tumult of Hong Kong, and features some of the finest hand-drawn backgrounds in anime.

Ghost in the Shell, 1995. DIR.: **Mamoru Oshii.** SCR.: **Kazunori Ito.** ART: **Hiromasa Ogura, Shuichi Kusamori.** ANI.: **Hiroyuki Okiura, Tensai Okamura, Toshihiko Nishikubo.** MUS.: **Kenji Kawai.** PRD.: **Production I.G. 83 mins.**

Ghost in the Shell is set in the year 2029, and takes place in the fictional New Port City. Many people are augmenting their bodies with technology, and a global electronic network now connects the world. The cyborg agent Major Motoko Kusanagi and her partner Batou are on the hunt for the mysterious Puppet Master who, like a computer virus, hacks into his victims' cybernetic brains.

The set was intended to be futuristic while still retaining a strong resemblance to the present – the original manga by Shirow Masamune was situated in a sprawling but obviously Japanese future metropolis. Whereas Tokyo is clearly recognizable as the location for the Patlabor films, the hybrid cityscape of *Ghost in the Shell* was largely inspired by Hong Kong. Mamoru Oshii recognized that Hong Kong, a city where tradition intersects with the latest high-tech developments, was the ideal model for his vision. For Oshii, old waterways and newly built high-rises symbolize the information flow that turns the city into a gigantic data space. He felt that the city of the near future will possess an element of the unknown – to achieve this uncanny quality, he sought to express the flood of information surging through this disparate environment.

New Port City is marked by a stark contrast between the old town and the recently built high-rise district. Locations in the old town are full of the traces left by former inhabitants, and are depicted with an almost documentary realism. In contrast, the new town appears sterile and technological. Art director Hiromasa Ogura was responsible for expressing this contrast between the two urban worlds in the film's artwork. As a result, cold blue tones dominate scenes set in the new town, whereas the old town is characterized by subdued lighting. In addition to the trips made by the official location-scouting photographer Haruhiko Higami, Ogura visited Hong Kong himself, capturing his impressions on film. He used these latter photos mostly to provide inspiration for the mood of the colours and lighting in the film. To incorporate the chaos of a Chinese old town and its inherent energy, Ogura tried to illustrate all the elements of each location in detail. This was a significant change from his previous work with Oshii on *Patlabor: The Movie* (1989) and *Patlabor 2: The Movie* (1993), in which he omitted objects in the shadows, or just sketched them in an abstract way.

Ghost in the Shell, cut no. 683
Final production background, *detail*
Hiromasa Ogura
Poster colour on paper
84 × 42 cm (33⅛ × 16⅝ in.)

The last cut of *Ghost in the Shell* presents an overview of New Port City, the location of the entire story. In the distance, the skyscrapers of the new town rise at the centre of an artificial island. These buildings are depicted as being around three hundred metres tall, with low-rise buildings filling the spaces around them. The high-rises in the foreground are a more conventional height, at around thirty storeys or so. Art director Hiromasa Ogura has suggested that this image expresses 'the coexistence of the old and the new', a central theme throughout the film (Oshii 1995b).

Oshii's approach on *Patlabor 2: The Movie* had shown a greater consciousness of photographic effects, and imitated the techniques of live-action films. In addition, the landscape played an important role in the story, with Shinjuku obviously providing the stage for the film. Even though *Ghost in the Shell*'s New Port City was modelled after Hong Kong, it is still a virtual set created for a movie – the urban vision for the two projects was fundamentally different.

Ghost in the Shell was largely shot on film, with digital effects only used in some cuts – mainly those that illustrate digital technologies. Depictions of screens, scanners, artificial intelligence and cyborg bodies did benefit from digital techniques, but the final production backgrounds by Hiromasa Ogura and Shuichi Kusamori are among the finest examples of hand-drawn craftsmanship in the anime industry, and have been recognized as the peak of this art.

Ghost in the Shell, cut no. 316
Final production background, book
Shuichi Kusamori
Two layers superimposed, poster colour on paper and cel
26 × 38 cm (10¼ × 15 in.)

In this cut, a water bus travels down a waterway that flows under an elevated road. Ships like this float slowly through the city, which is buried under bright signs and thick crowds.

This is the third cut of a scene in which Major Kusanagi, the main protagonist, wanders through the city, exploring the space around her but also searching for meaning inside herself (cuts nos 314–46, approx. 3:10 mins).

The sequence occurs in the middle of the film's running time, and also at the midpoint of the story. Oshii prefers to place such sequences at his film's midpoints – similar scenes can be found in *Patlabor: The Movie* (1989), *Patlabor 2: The Movie* (1993) and *Innocence* (2004). It is shown almost entirely from the protagonist's point of view, therefore the backgrounds take the starring role and are rendered in great detail. During this scene, day turns into night and it starts raining, which creates a dream-like impression. The first part, which shows the old town in daylight, was executed by Shuichi Kusamori, while the latter part – the cityscape at night and in heavy rain – was drawn by Hiromasa Ogura.

Ghost in the Shell, cut no. 318
Final production background, book
Shuichi Kusamori
Two layers superimposed, poster colour on paper and cel
26 × 38 cm (10¼ × 15 in.)

Water plays an important role in this sequence. In the first part, the camera often hovers on a vessel skimming over the waterway's surface. In the second part, the camera observes the falling rain. Water symbolizes the subconscious, with its surface acting as the threshold into consciousness, into the light of day. Major Kusanagi ponders her identity while moving slowly through the densely packed urban space.

Ghost in the Shell, cut no. 316
Still image

Ghost in the Shell
Location scouting
Haruhiko Higami
Black-and-white photography, small-format negative

Haruhiko Higami began working with Oshii on *Patlabor: The Movie* (1989). Higami's role in production design is similar to that of a location scout on a live-action film. After the initial storyboards for a film have been produced, Higami's task is to find and photograph real cityscapes that underpin the film's vision. His photographs inform the design work of the concept and layout artists, and help to make their imaginative compositions more plausible.

Atsushi Takeuchi, the layout designer for *Ghost in the Shell*, found that 'there is a clear contrast between the old town and the new town, the two never achieve a fusion. It feels as if the inhabitants of the old town cling onto their lives under the pressure of modernization' (Oshii 1995b). In particular, there are great clusters of signboards everywhere – these advertisements, all executed in Chinese lettering, play an important role in the film's representation of New Port as a city immersed in and flooded by information.

Ghost in the Shell
Location scouting
Haruhiko Higami
Black-and-white photography, small-format negative

Ghost in the Shell
Location scouting
Haruhiko Higami
Black-and-white photography, small-format negative

Ghost in the Shell, cut no. 334
Final production background
Hiromasa Ogura
Poster colour on paper
27 × 38 cm (10¾ × 15 in.)

In the previous cut, it starts raining and daylight is gradually turning into night. From this cut onwards, Ogura drew the final production backgrounds for the sequence. This image features signboards protruding like tentacles from a deformed building. The impression of these signs reaching out into the space of the old town in all directions is further emphasized by the use of a wide-angle lens.

Ghost in the Shell, cut no. 334
Still image

Ghost in the Shell, cut no. 334
Layout
Atsushi Takeuchi
Pencil on paper
27 × 38 cm (10¾ × 15 in.)

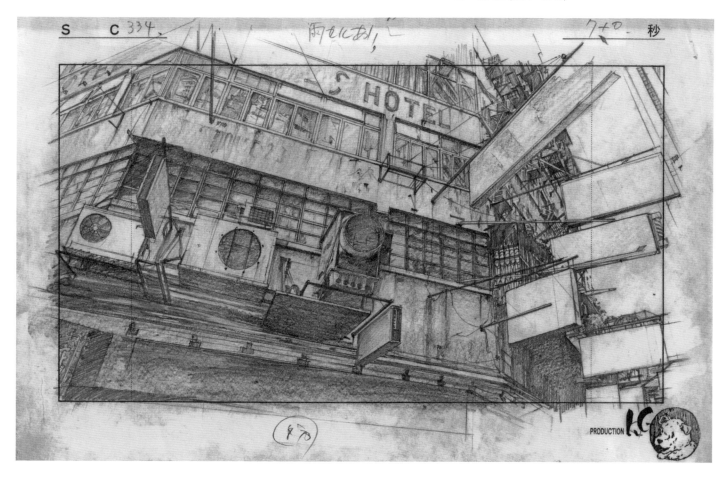

Ghost in the Shell, cut no. 335
Final production background, book
Hiromasa Ogura
Three layers superimposed, poster colour on paper and cel
27 × 42 cm (10¾ × 16⅝ in.)

Ghost in the Shell, cut no. 335
Still image

100   Ghost in the Shell

Ghost in the Shell, cut no. 335, base layer
Poster colour on paper
27 × 38 cm (10¾ × 15 in.)

Ghost in the Shell, cut no. 335, book 1
Poster colour on paper
17 × 42 cm (6¾ × 16⅝ in.)

The bridge is painted on a paper cut-out.

Ghost in the Shell, cut no. 335, book 2
Poster colour on cel
26 × 42 cm (10¼ × 16⅝ in.)

Hiromasa Ogura makes deft use of rough brush strokes to suggest detailing. In this piece, his artistry can best be observed in the texture of the traffic signal's metal frame.

Ghost in the Shell, cut no. 338
Still image

Ghost in the Shell, cut no. 338
Final production background, book
Hiromasa Ogura
Two layers superimposed, poster colour on paper and cel
27 × 38 cm (10¾ × 15 in.)

A sloping street washed by rainwater. Layout artist Atsushi Takeuchi placed the camera in an unusually low position in this cut, as if to suggest that the water is flowing directly onto the viewer.

102   Ghost in the Shell

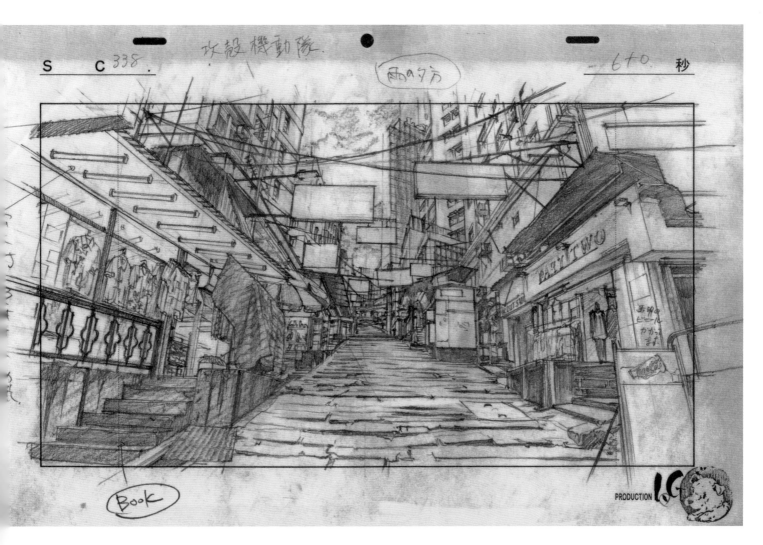

Ghost in the Shell, cut no. 338
Layout
Atsushi Takeuchi
Pencil on paper
27 × 38 cm (10¾ × 15 in.)

Ghost in the Shell, cut no. 341
Final production background
Hiromasa Ogura
Poster colour on paper
27 × 38 cm (10¾ × 15 in.)

The layout of this cut is virtually identical to the photograph taken by Haruhiko Higami, and the result looks almost as if it has been shot on location. Much of the realism of *Ghost in the Shell* derives from this approach to film-making.

Ghost in the Shell, cut no. 341
Still image

Ghost in the Shell
Location scouting
Haruhiko Higami
Black-and-white photography, small-format negative

Higami served as the location photographer on the production of *Ghost in the Shell*. His city views were collected on several trips to Hong Kong, and are the basis for the images of the old city in the film. Many of his photographs were incorporated almost directly into the movie, being drawn and painted to produce the background pictures. The photographs are monochrome to avoid hampering the art director and colour designer's choice of palette for the project.

Ghost in the Shell
Location scouting
Hiromasa Ogura
Colour photography, small-format negatives

Ogura went into an air-conditioned shop with his camera. When he came back out into the humid, sultry night, the camera lens misted up. The resulting images show large halos around the lights. This haziness inspired Ogura in the design of the image boards and backgrounds.

Ghost in the Shell, cut no. 342
Final production background, book
Hiromasa Ogura
Three layers superimposed, poster colour on paper and cel
27 × 38 cm (10¾ × 15 in.)

This cut quotes a similar view in *Blade Runner* (1982), which also features a floating advertisement vehicle. Many of the special effects and lighting effects in *Ghost in the Shell* were superimposed onto photographic film by means of multiple exposures. Hisao Shirai, who was responsible for the photography for the project, had an especially hard time on this particular cut. Because the picture includes reflections of the advertising vessel in many of the surrounding glass surfaces, he had to rewind and superimpose the photographic image with different effect layers up to fourteen times in order to achieve one frame of film (Oshii 1995b).

Ghost in the Shell, cut no. 342
Still image

108　　Ghost in the Shell

Ghost in the Shell, cut no. 342
Layout
Atsushi Takeuchi
Pencil on paper
27 × 38 cm (10¾ × 15 in.)

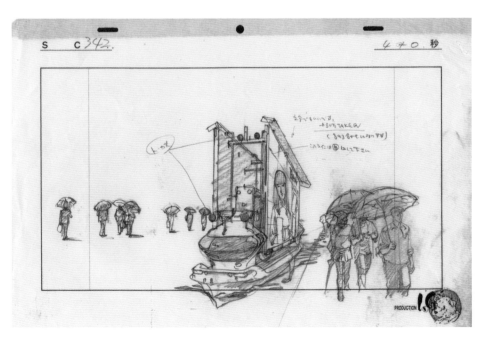

Ghost in the Shell, cut no. 342
Layout
Atsushi Takeuchi
Pencil on paper
27 × 38 cm (10¾ × 15 in.)

In this cut, the float is placed in the background, and thus is drawn by the art team instead of the animation team, who would usually be responsible for any animated objects.

Ghost in the Shell, cut no. 344
Final production background, book
Hiromasa Ogura
Two layers superimposed, poster colour on paper and cel
27 × 38 cm (10¾ × 15 in.)

110 Ghost in the Shell

Ghost in the Shell, cut no. 345
Final production background, book
Hiromasa Ogura
Two layers superimposed, poster colour on paper and cel
27 × 38 cm (10¾ × 15 in.)

This cut depicts the same location as the previous one (cut no. 344 opposite). The latter features a bird's-eye view, following the rain drops as they fall onto the surfaces below. In cut no. 345, the point of interest – a display of mannequins in a shop window – is depicted from a very low angle, as if the camera is floating on the surface of the water. The boat is painted on cel so that it can sway slightly up and down on the water.

Ghost in the Shell
Image board
Hiromasa Ogura
Poster colour on paper
25.5 × 36 cm (10⅛ × 14¼ in.)

Based on his own photographic documentation of Hong Kong, Ogura painted these image boards of the cityscape by day and night (opposite). The director, Mamoru Oshii, wanted a detailed and visually complex set, so the final backgrounds are much richer in detail. This daylight view was used as an image board for the final production background of cut no. 155, but the night view was not used further.

　Ogura notes that 'there is a difference between the old and the new town in the accumulation of years passed. In the old town, whether it's a dirty wall or a sticky poster, it's a landscape that has been shaped over many years. Therefore, the appearance of the city and the huge amount of information contained in it represent the long history of the city itself' (Oshii 1995b).

112　Ghost in the Shell

Ghost in the Shell
Image board
Hiromasa Ogura
Poster colour on paper
25.5 × 36 cm (10⅛ × 14¼ in.)

Ghost in the Shell, cut no. 155
Still image

An armoured van drives by the waterway. A small boat floats in the water channel. The huge buildings of the new town dominate this view.

Ghost in the Shell, cut no. 160
Final production background
Shuichi Kusamori
Poster colour on paper
27 × 38 cm (10¾ × 15 in.)

The following four production backgrounds (cuts nos 160, 161, 168 and 178) are used to create a shot-reverse-shot sequence in a narrow street. The scene is framed by the old town on one side and the skyline of the new town – the location for the impending escalation of the plot – on the other. In both directions, the camera positions change in height and also move further into the space.

Ghost in the Shell, cut no. 160
Still image

114   Ghost in the Shell

Ghost in the Shell, cut no. 161
Still image

Ghost in the Shell, cut no. 161
Final production background
Shuichi Kusamori
Poster colour on paper
27 × 38 cm (10¾ × 15 in.)

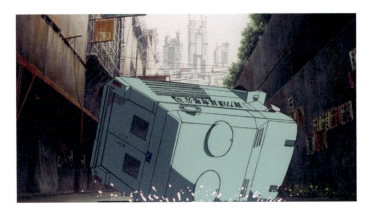

Ghost in the Shell, cut no. 168
Still image

The van depicted in cut no. 155 (see p. 112) is brought to a violent halt in a narrow street in the old town.

Ghost in the Shell, cut no. 168
Final production background
Shuichi Kusamori
Poster colour on paper
27 × 38 cm (10¾ × 15 in.)

Ghost in the Shell, cut no. 178
Final production background
Shuichi Kusamori
Poster colour on paper
27 × 38 cm (10¾ × 15 in.)

Ghost in the Shell, cut no. 178
Still image

Ghost in the Shell
Location scouting
Haruhiko Higami
Black-and-white photography,
small-format negatives

Ghost in the Shell, cut no. 195
Final production background
Shuichi Kusamori
Poster colour on paper
46 × 42 cm (18⅛ × 16⅝ in.)

This image shows Major Kusanagi's view as she looks down on the market, the location for the next action sequence. In these backgrounds, piles of containers, rows of signs and accumulated products fill up the entire space. Atsushi Takeuchi, the supervising layout artist, points out that it is important 'to draw without restraint in such a case. The effect needs to be overwhelming, just from a quick glance, so the person who draws this scene needs to be enthusiastic. It may be frustrating that only a small part of the information will be consciously transmitted to the audience but, when amassed together, this excess of visual information creates the sensation of a rich, vibrant world. In order to express the intensity that Asian cities possess today, there is no other choice but to draw a lot of detail' (Oshii 1995b).

Kusamori worked on most of the production backgrounds for the market scene. He describes himself as an illustrator who 'usually draws in a little bit too much detail'. He just 'cannot stop adding detail until the entire page is covered' (Kusamori, personal interview, 2019). His approach suited this particular scene perfectly.

Ghost in the Shell, cut no. 196
Final production background
Hiromasa Ogura
Poster colour on paper
27 × 38 cm (10¾ × 15 in.)

Although Kusamori drew most of the final production backgrounds for the market scene, Ogura also worked on a few, including this one. The camera angle is similar to cut no. 212 (opposite), which was executed by Kusamori. When comparing both pieces, the differences in the artists' renderings of the scene become obvious – the treatment of textures in the background is especially distinct. While Kusamori tends to add lots of detail, Ogura employs a flatter texture. The fast-paced action taking place in the foreground smooths out this stylistic difference between the two backdrops.

Ghost in the Shell, cut no. 196
Still image

120　Ghost in the Shell

Ghost in the Shell, cut no. 212
Final production background
Shuichi Kusamori
Poster colour on paper
27 × 38 cm (10¾ × 15 in.)

Ghost in the Shell, cut no. 212
Still image

The villain uses a 'thermoptic camouflage suit' in this scene, and only appears as a phantom, causing turmoil on the market street.

Ghost in the Shell, cut no. 202
Final production background
Shuichi Kusamori
Poster colour on paper
27 × 38 cm (10¾ × 15 in.)

According to *Ghost in the Shell*'s director, Mamoru Oshii, 'There are places that are cluttered. If you don't express all that detail, you cannot make the audience imagine life there. It needs to be a whirlpool of overflowing information. Otherwise it is impossible to express the weird energy inside a place such as New Port City' (Oshii 1995b).

Ghost in the Shell, cut no. 188
Final production background
Shuichi Kusamori
Poster colour on paper
27 × 38 cm (10¾ × 15 in.)

This shot presents a narrow back alley behind the market. The perspective is challenging because the camera is off-centre. The layout needs to assume three vanishing points in order to render the space accurately.

Ghost in the Shell, cut no. 228
Final production background
Shuichi Kusamori
Poster colour on paper
40 × 36 cm (15¾ × 14¼ in.)

In contrast to the Patlabor films, *Ghost in the Shell* focuses almost exclusively on the depiction of the built environment – the sky is rarely visible. As a result, both Patlabor films convey an open sensation due to their visible horizons, while *Ghost in the Shell* feels much more closed in.

Ghost in the Shell, cut no. 231
Final production background
Shuichi Kusamori
Poster colour on paper
36 × 40 cm (14¼ × 15¾ in.)

Ghost in the Shell
Location scouting
Haruhiko Higami
Black-and-white photography,
small-format negative

Ghost in the Shell, cut no. 239
Final production background
Shuichi Kusamori
Poster colour on paper
27 × 38 cm (10¾ × 15 in.)

A group of buildings, each hundreds of storeys high, towers over a dark back alley in the old town. This cut frames the cluster of high-rises at the alley's end, and depicts a shaft of light spilling in from the outside world. The image was laid out with the idea of a telephoto lens in mind, compressing the screen. In effect, the visual and symbolic distance between the new town and the old town is shortened (Oshii 1995b).

Ghost in the Shell, cut no. 239
Still image

Ghost in the Shell, cut no. 240
Image board
Hiromasa Ogura
Poster colour on paper
25.5 × 36cm (10⅛ × 14¼ in.)

Compared to the final production background, this image board drawn by Ogura at the beginning of the production process seems to be comparatively sober, rather than extravagantly detailed. Oshii requested that the visual density be intensified to create the cluttered urban tapestry he desired.

Ghost in the Shell, cut no. 240
Final production background
Shuichi Kusamori
Poster colour on paper
27 × 38 cm (10¾ × 15 in.)

This cut shows the back alley, which the villain has just left, from the direction of the new town (see cut no. 239, pp. 126–27). It seems as if the old town is buried under billboards, with their rich textures covering the entirety of its walls.

    Chased by Major Kusanagi, the villain has finally found a way out of the narrow alleys of the old town. He reaches an open space just in front of the river and gazes towards the new town on the opposite side of the water.

Ghost in the Shell, cut no. 248
Final production background
Shuichi Kusamori
Poster colour on paper
27 × 38 cm (10¾ × 15 in.)

A complete view of the close-up of cut no. 240 (opposite).

Ghost in the Shell, cut no. 243
Final production background
Hiromasa Ogura
Poster colour on paper
27 × 38 cm (10¾ × 15 in.)

The skyline of the new town as seen from the edge of the old town. This ensemble of buildings has already appeared in several earlier scenes, most recently in cut no. 239 (see pp. 126–27), before being revealed in its entirety in this shot.

For Ogura, the new town was difficult to capture. It is almost a mirage – a world in which only buildings seem to exist, indifferent towards the existence of the people who live there. Ogura attests to the excellence of the layout drawn by Takashi Watabe for this section of the film. However, even with the plethora of detail in this layout, he still didn't know what kind of building materials were to be used and how the textures should feel. Finally he decided that the new town should appear sterile when compared to the drab, dirty tones of the old town.

Ghost in the Shell, cut no. 243
Still image

Ghost in the Shell, cut no. 243
Layout
Takashi Watabe
Pencil on paper
25 × 35 cm (9⅞ × 13⅞ in.)

Takashi Watabe's drawings were used as blueprints for Hiromasa Ogura's background paintings. Each layout was submitted to Mamoru Oshii. The latter's characteristic seal with its dog's head cleared the drawing for the next step of the production. Part of the detail of this layout could not be transferred to the final production background.

Ghost in the Shell, cut no. 477
Base layer
Poster colour on paper
27 × 38 cm (10¾ × 15 in.)

Ghost in the Shell, cut no. 477
Book, layer 1
Poster colour on cel
27 × 38 cm (10¾ × 15 in.)

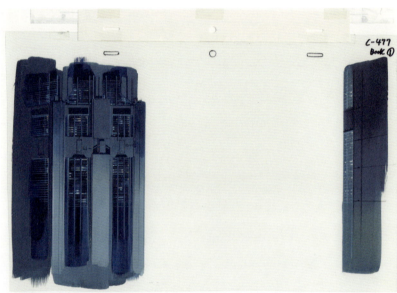

Ghost in the Shell, cut no. 477
Book, layer 2
Poster colour on cel
25.5 × 39 cm (10⅛ × 15⅜ in.)

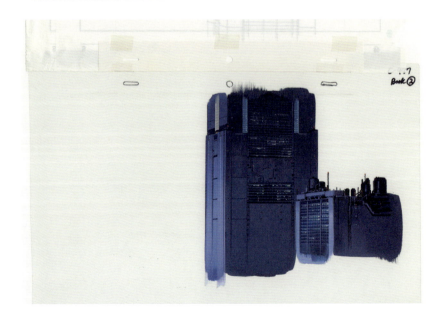

Ghost in the Shell, cut no. 477
Final production background, book
Hiromasa Ogura
Three layers, poster colour on paper and cel
Digital montage
27 × 38 cm (10¾ × 15 in.)

This composition is based on a layout by Takashi Watabe (see Riekeles 2011, p. 110). Three layers are superimposed onto each other and moved very slowly at different speeds during the animation process. The background plane, middle layer and top layer are all shifted to the right but at different speeds, with the paper background moving slowest and the transparent top layer moving fastest.

Although the perspective of the building itself does not change, the animation of the layers creates a sense of spatial depth, as if the camera is moving in space. This 'pseudo-movement' produces a sensation that is completely different from live action or from 3DCG animation. This specific sense of movement is unique to cel animation.

Ghost in the Shell, cut no. 477
Still image

Ghost in the Shell, cut no. 509
Final production background
Hiromasa Ogura
Poster colour on paper
27 × 38 cm (10¾ × 15 in.)

The photographer for *Ghost in the Shell*, Hisao Shirai, decided after several tests with different films to use Kodak 5293 stock, which has a greater sensitivity (ISO 200) than more conventional films (ISO 50–125). This was especially important in capturing dark areas in the images, which are a prevalent motif in this production. Using customary film stocks would have resulted in a tendency for darker colours to fade into black. This choice also allowed him to make use of several filters, including polarization filters, to make cel scratches less noticeable.

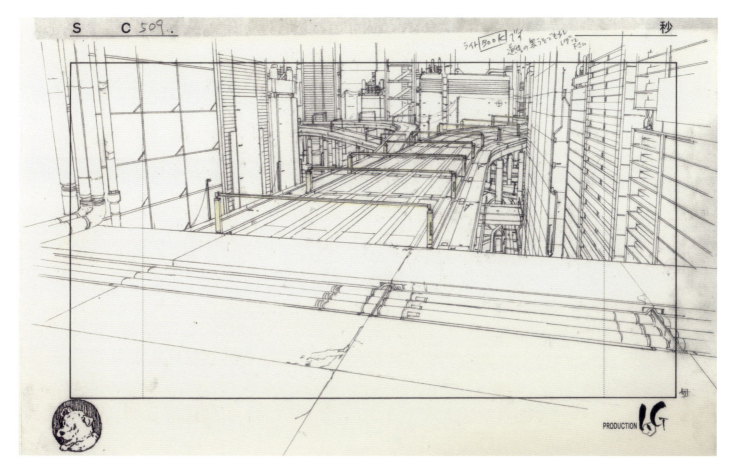

Ghost in the Shell, cut no. 509
Layout
Takashi Watabe
Pencil on paper
25 × 35 cm (9⅞ × 13⅞ in.)

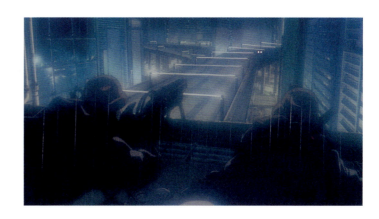

Ghost in the Shell, cut no. 509
Still image

METROPOLIS

Based on the manga by the legendary artist Osamu Tezuka, *Metropolis* combines traditional, paper-based animation with a digital workflow, employing this duality to express ongoing conflicts between humanity and technological progress.

Metropolis, 2001 (English title: Robotic Angel). DIR.: Rintaro. SCR.: Katsuhiro Otomo. ART: Shuichi Kusamori. ANI.: Yasuhiro Nakura. MUS.: Toshiyuki Honda. PRD.: Madhouse, Tezuka Pro. 107 mins.

Metropolis is based on the manga of the same title by Osamu Tezuka, first published in 1949. As in Fritz Lang's classic silent film *Metropolis* (1927), Tezuka's story deals with the conflict between humanity and technological progress. In the futuristic city of Metropolis, humans and robots coexist, but live in well-defined spaces. Japanese detective Ban arrives in the city, accompanied by his nephew Kenichi. Their mission is to arrest scientist Dr Laughton, who is accused of organ-trafficking. Dr Laughton works for the most powerful man in the city, Duke Red, who uses the services of the scientist to create an ultra-modern robot with the appearance of his late daughter, Tima. This robot is the key to a secret weapon that has been designed to secure the domination of the world – the Ziggurat, a tall tower in the image of the Tower of Babel. Following the assassination of Dr Laughton, Tima finds herself lost in the gigantic city. She meets Kenichi, with whom she escapes many dangers. Kenichi does not want to let Tima turn into a cold, domineering automaton who destroys the human species. Together, Tima and Kenichi try to overcome their daunting fates.

Metropolis was produced by the founder of the Madhouse animation studio, Masao Maruyama, who also produced films by the talented director Satoshi Kon. It features art by some of the finest artists in Tokyo's anime industry. The screenplay was written by Katsuhiro Otomo, who has acknowledged his admiration for Tezuka's work. When Tezuka began writing *Metropolis*, he had not seen Lang's movie, but was inspired by a magazine article about the silent classic to imagine what life would be like in a city of the future (Clements & McCarthy 2015, p. 528). This is the main reason why his story is only loosely inspired by Lang's original film – in many ways, the latter's influence seems to be stronger in Otomo's *AKIRA* (1988) than in this production, despite the fact that the two films have the same title.

Metropolis shares many similarities with *AKIRA*, such as a city terrorized by a group that is secretly funded by a corrupt politician; a great construction venture with a hidden purpose; and a child unaware that it has the power to destroy the world. The film was originally scheduled for an American release in late 2001, but was delayed for several months due to the terrorist attack on New York on 11 September – during the film's explosive finale, most of Metropolis's architecture is destroyed.

Metropolis,
scene 49, cut no. 17
Final production background,
detail
Shuichi Kusamori
Poster colour on paper
26 × 43 cm (10¼ × 17 in.)

View into Zone –1, the first underground level of Metropolis. The scenes taking place in the lower parts of Metropolis are animated against hand-drawn, paper-based backgrounds, while the scenes above ground level have 3DCG backdrops.

Metropolis is, like *Innocence* (2004) and *Tekkonkinkreet* (2006), a hybrid production combining traditional, paper-based animation and a digital workflow. However, the producers did not aim to integrate the former into the latter but rather employed both means of film-making in order to achieve distinguishable aesthetics for different parts of the set. The city of Metropolis is composed of two layers, the lower and the higher city, corresponding with Lang's vision. These two areas of the city are animated in different ways. The higher city's architecture is rendered in 3DCG, while the lower city's caverns and infrastructure are drawn with poster colour on paper.

Shuichi Kusamori, the art director, conceived of the higher city – the realm of humans – as a largely rectangular and polygonal world, which could therefore be easily produced with 3D software. The preliminary sketches and layouts for this region were devised by Takashi Watabe, and were drawn with pencil on paper and subsequently worked out digitally. The lower part of the city is the realm of robots, a counter-world to the surface, and is softer and more organic in both its ambience and the quality of its surfaces. Kusamori took charge of these designs himself, executing the final production backgrounds in considerable detail. During this production, Kusamori developed the digital skills that he would later employ to great acclaim on *Innocence* (Kusamori, personal interview, June 2019).

Metropolis, scene 10, cuts nos 12, 19 and 21
Concept design
Takashi Watabe
Pencil on paper
23.4 × 35.8 cm (9¼ × 14⅛ in.)

Takashi Watabe designed the sets and layouts for most of the scenes in *Metropolis* that take place above ground level. Scene 10 at the very beginning of the film highlights the city and its buildings. The shots are arranged as an exposition of the film's urban world, with the protagonists walking through the streets and discussing the adventure that they are about to embark upon.

The main setting is a plaza in front of a theatre building (scene 10, cut no. 10, see pp. 140–43). To design the layouts for cuts 12, 19 and 21 (see pp. 144–48), which occur in front of this building, Watabe fixed the exact camera positions on this map. Following the camera's perspective and the architectural concepts, he then created the blueprints for the background design.

Translation of the annotations (from left to right): 'Building in the centre of cut 19'; 'Camera position for cuts 12 and 19, both in front of the theatre building (Robotrevue)'; 'Building with triangular windows'; 'Close-up of camera position of cut 21, the three protagonists directly facing the camera (Robotrevue)'.

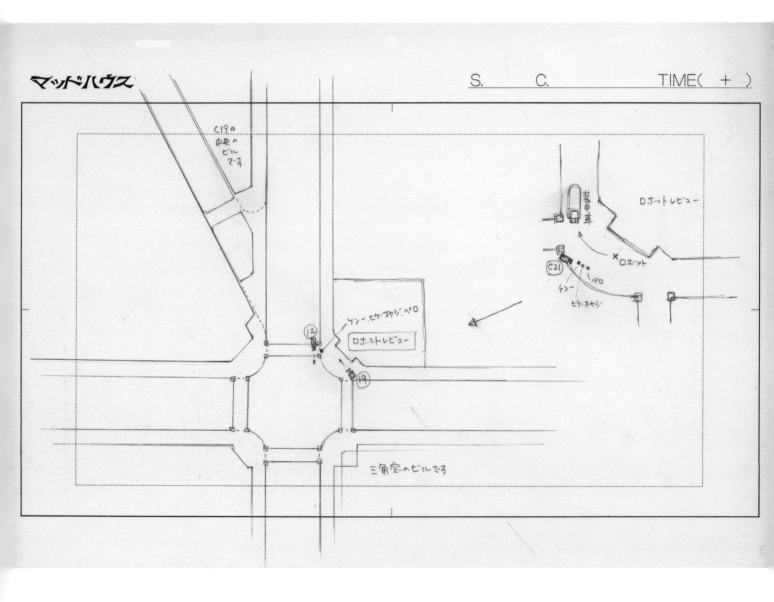

Metropolis, scene 10
Concept design
Takashi Watabe
Pencil on paper
35.8 × 23.4 cm (14⅛ × 9¼ in.)

Design of the theatre, the main background element of scene 10. In his concept layout (see p. 139), Watabe uses the name 'Robotrevue' to refer to this theatre, but the title 'Radio City Paradise' was used in the final film.

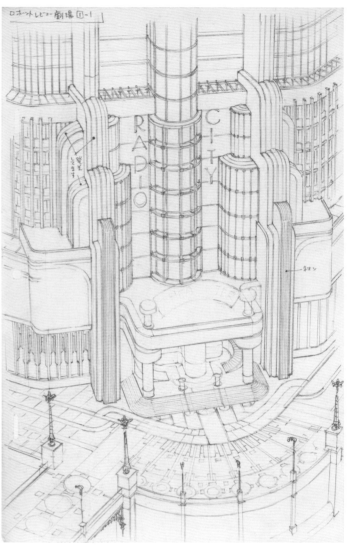

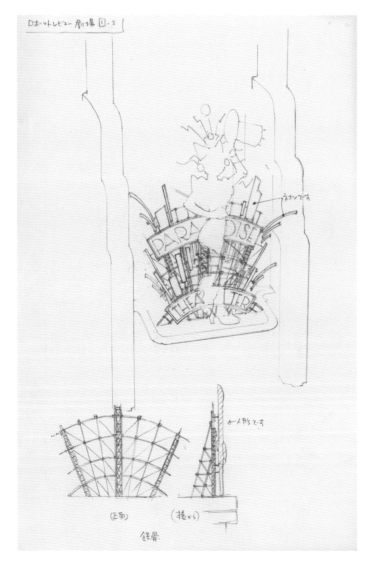

Metropolis, scene 10
Concept design
Takashi Watabe
Pencil on paper
35.8 × 23.4 cm (14⅛ × 9¼ in.)

Concept for Radio City Paradise's signboard. This needed to be a separate element because it falls off the building in the following cuts.

Metropolis, scene 10
Concept design
Takashi Watabe
Pencil on paper
23.4 × 35.8 cm (9¼ × 14⅛ in.)

Concept for the canopy of Radio City Paradise.

Metropolis, scene 10, cut no. 10
Still images

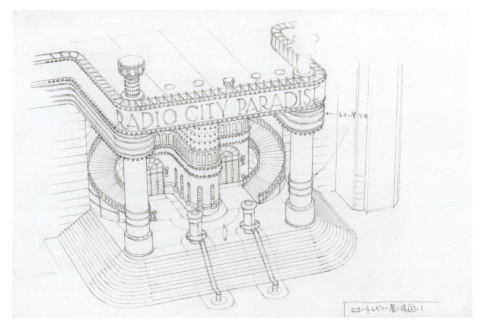

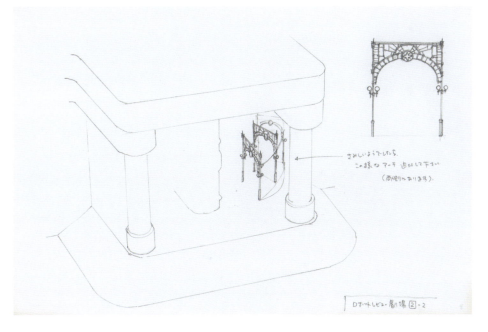

Metropolis, scene 10
Concept design
Takashi Watabe
Pencil on paper
23.4 × 35.8 cm (9¼ × 14⅛ in.)

Concept for the lighting of the staircase under the canopy.

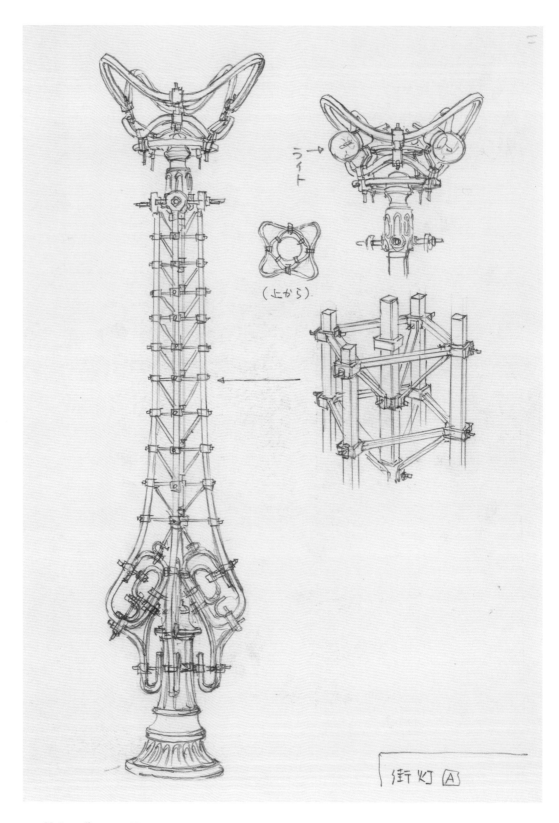

Metropolis, scene 10
Concept design
Takashi Watabe
Pencil on paper
26 × 18.5 cm (10¼ × 7⅜ in.)

Concept design for the large street lights in front of the theatre building, with their strong Art Nouveau influences.

Metropolis, scene 10
Concept design
Takashi Watabe
Pencil on paper
23.4 × 35.8 cm (9¼ × 14⅛ in.)

Concept design for other street lights in the rest of scene 10.

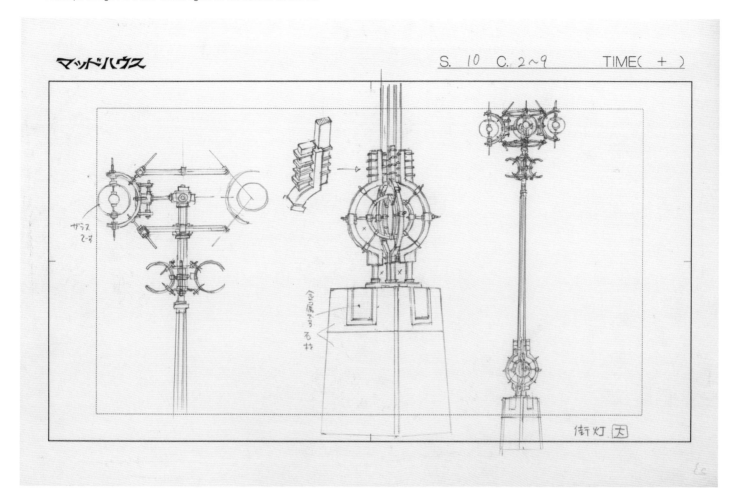

Metropolis, scene 10
Concept design
Takashi Watabe
Pencil on paper
23.4 × 35.8 cm (9¼ × 14⅛ in.)

Takashi Watabe designed details of the cityscape, including these handrails along the sidewalk. The composition and functioning of these elements had to be explicit in order to transmit sufficient information to allow the 3DCG department to model the structures.

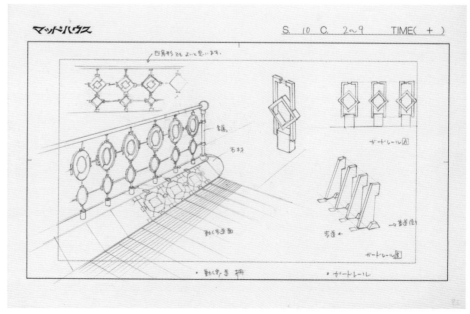

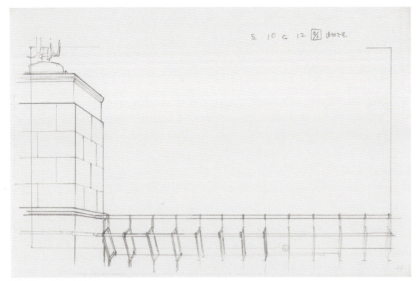

Metropolis, scene 10, cut no. 12
Layout, 0/3
Takashi Watabe
Pencil on paper
23.4 × 35.8 cm (9¼ × 14⅛ in.)

In most cases, Watabe arranged the thee-dimensional space of the cityscape into distinct layers to allow for additional lighting effects. This also enhanced the sense of spatial depth. Here in cut no. 12, the set has been divided into five different layers to achieve this impression.

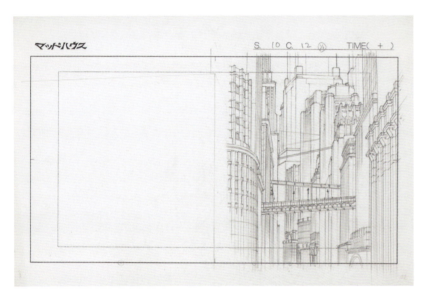

Metropolis, scene 10, cut no. 12
Layout, 1/3
Takashi Watabe
Pencil on paper
23.4 × 35.8 cm (9¼ × 14⅛ in.)

This layout is an alternative version to layouts 1/3 B1 and B2, which were the ones finally used. The difference between these two designs provides a good sense of the director's artistic vision for *Metropolis* and the enormous amount of detail in the design of the sets.

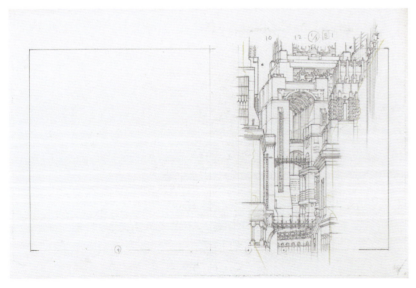

Metropolis, scene 10, cut no. 12
Layout, 1/3 B1
Takashi Watabe
Pencil on paper
23.4 × 35.8 cm (9¼ × 14⅛ in.)

Final layout of the middleground on the right side.

Metropolis, scene 10, cut no. 12
Still image

Metropolis, scene 10, cut no. 12
Layout, 1/3 B2
Takashi Watabe
Pencil on paper
23.4 × 35.8 cm (9¼ × 14⅛ in.)

Second layer of the middleground on the right side.

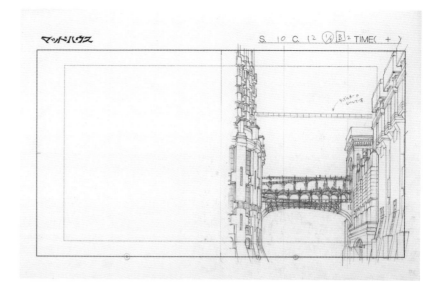

Metropolis, scene 10, cut no. 12
Layout, 2/3
Takashi Watabe
Pencil on paper
23.4 × 35.8 cm (9¼ × 14⅛ in.)

Middleground left side.

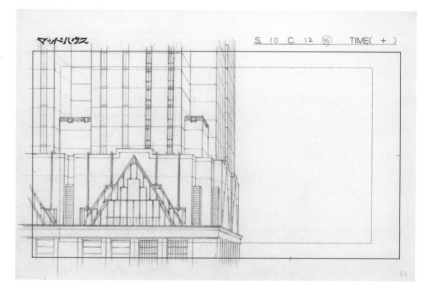

Metropolis, scene 10, cut no. 12
Layout, 3/3
Takashi Watabe
Pencil on paper
23.4 × 35.8 cm (9¼ × 14⅛ in.)

Foreground layer with the lamps as designed in the concept (see p. 142).

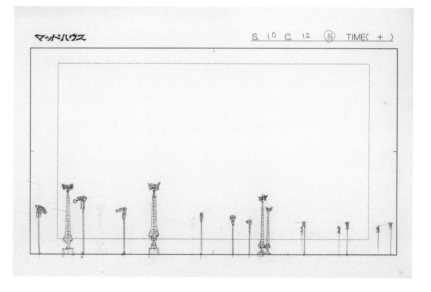

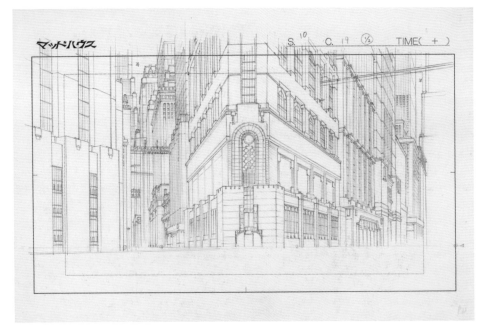

Metropolis, scene 10, cut no. 19
Layout, 1/2 #1
Takashi Watabe
Pencil on paper
23.4 × 35.8 cm (9¼ × 14⅛ in.)

This cut is divided into three layers: background, middleground and foreground. The horizon line near the bottom edge of the drawing defines the height of the camera. Below that line, the background is not visible in the final image.

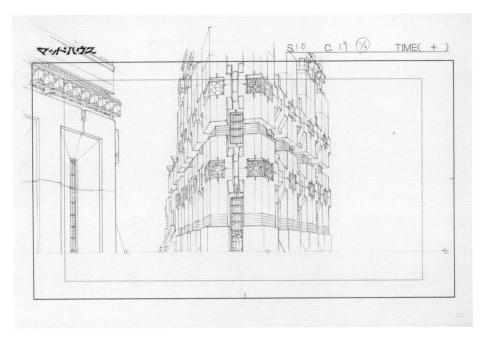

Metropolis, scene 10, cut no. 19
Layout, 1/2 #2
Takashi Watabe
Pencil on paper
23.4 × 35.8 cm (9¼ × 14⅛ in.)

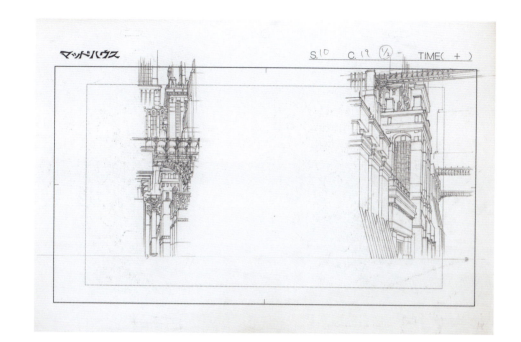

Metropolis, scene 10, cut no. 19
Layout, 1/2, alternative
Takashi Watabe
Pencil on paper
23.4 × 35.8 cm (9¼ × 14⅛ in.)

This layout is an alternative version to layouts 1/2 #1 and 1/2 #2, but was not realized as a production background.

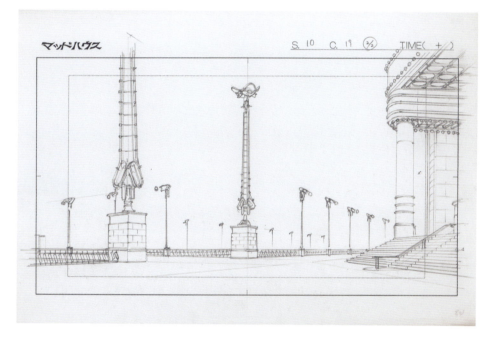

Metropolis, scene 10, cut no. 19
Layout, 2/2
Takashi Watabe
Pencil on paper
23.4 × 35.8 cm (9¼ × 14⅛ in.)

The street lamps in front of the theatre's canopy (see p. 141).

Metropolis, scene 10, cut no. 19
Still image

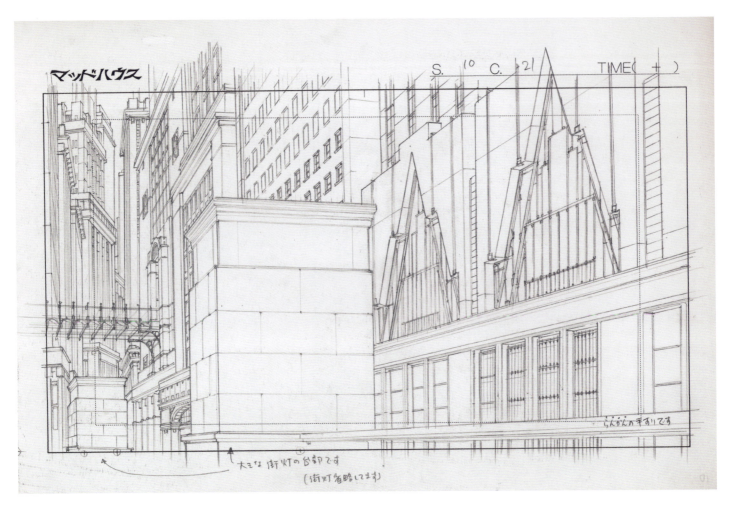

Metropolis, scene 10, cut no. 21
Layout
Takashi Watabe
Pencil on paper
23.4 × 35.8 cm (9¼ × 14⅛ in.)

Compared to cuts nos 12 and 19 (see pp. 144–47), this layout is quite straightforward, with one layer holding enough information for the entire cut. The plinth serves as a platform for a street lantern.

Metropolis, scene 10, cut no. 21
Still image

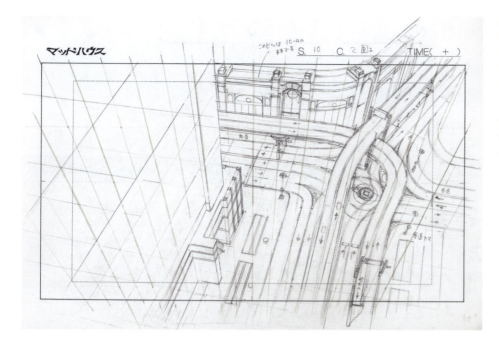

Metropolis, scene 10, cut no. 2
Layout, B1
Takashi Watabe
Pencil on paper
23.4 × 35.8 cm (9¼ × 14⅛ in.)

Bird's-eye view down onto a street in Metropolis. The highway is drawn on a separate layer to allow for special lighting effects and for the animation of the moving cars.

Metropolis, scene 10, cut no. 2
Layout, B2
Takashi Watabe
Pencil on paper
23.4 × 35.8 cm (9¼ × 14⅛ in.)

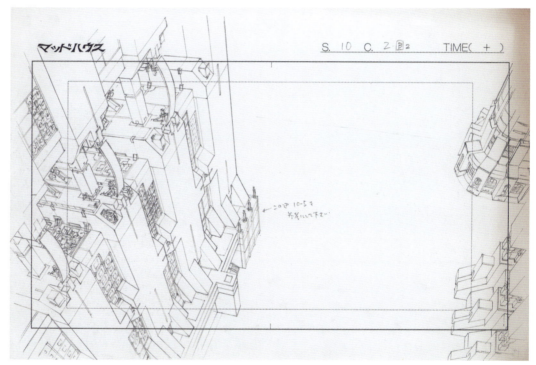

Metropolis, scene 10, cut no. 2
Still image

Metropolis, scene 12, cut no. 7 et al.
Layout
Shuichi Kusamori
Fine liner on paper
50 × 70.7 cm (19¾ × 27⅞ in.)

Kusamori created the layout and the final production background for this view (see pp. 152–53). His style is characterized by the inclusion of a large amount of detail.

Metropolis, scene 12, cut no. 7 et al.
Final production background
Shuichi Kusamori
Poster colour on paper
50 × 70.7 cm (19¾ × 27⅞ in.)

Kusamori worked for two weeks on this large tableau, which was used in several cuts. Sometimes only a portion is visible, thus the illustration needed to be rich in detail. It depicts a section through the lower town of Metropolis, Zone −1. Pipes, vents and other components convey a sense of being at the heart of the city's infrastructure.

Metropolis, scene 12, cut no. 6 et al.
Final production background
Shuichi Kusamori
Poster colour on paper
26 × 43 cm (10¼ × 17 in.)

This production background presents the first level of the city's underground, Zone −1. It was used in several cuts, usually with only a section visible. To fill the screen, it too had to be executed in great detail.

Metropolis, scene 12, cut no. 6
Still image

154   Metropolis

Metropolis, scene 38, cut no. 1
Final production background
Shuichi Kusamori
Poster colour on paper
26 × 43 cm (10¼ × 17 in.)

The opening shot of the entrance to Zone -2, the power-plant zone. The division of the screen into two highly distinct layers to create a sense of depth, with a red hue in the foreground and a bright green colour at the back, is bold and unusual. Two characters, the size of grains of rice, come walking in from the left-hand side of the bridge.

Metropolis, scene 37, cut no. 2
Final production background
Shuichi Kusamori
Poster colour on paper and digital effect
26 × 43 cm (10¼ × 17 in.)

Kusamori painted this final production background with poster colour on paper and then retouched it digitally to create the flare effect.

INNOCENCE

Renowned for the exceptional quality of its 'Chinese Gothic' cityscapes, *Innocence* is a pivotal project in the digital transformation of the animation process, and was also the first anime to be nominated for the Palme d'Or at the Cannes Film Festival.

Innocence, 2004 (English title: Ghost in the Shell 2: Innocence). DIR.: **Mamoru Oshii.** SCR.: **Mamoru Oshii.** ART: **Shuichi Kusamori (credited as Shuichi Hirata).** ANI.: **Hiroyuki Okiura, Kazuchika Kise.** MUS.: **Kenji Kawai.** PRD.: **Production I.G. 98 mins.**

Innocence continues the *Ghost in the Shell* saga. Set in the year 2032, it follows detectives Batou and Togusa as they investigate a series of murders committed by malfunctioning 'gynoids' (fembots). As the story unfolds, the motive becomes more apparent: the gynoids are being given human sentiences stolen from young women in order to make them appear more realistic, and are then attempting to free themselves from their owners. The film deals with the ethics of artificial intelligence and the vulnerability of our networked systems to manipulation. *Innocence* draws on an original manga by Masamune Shirow, but the script is largely the work of Mamoru Oshii.

The vision for the urban setting in *Innocence* is more abstracted than that for *Ghost in the Shell* (1995). Its production design references the pre-industrial Southeast-Asian mainland, yet high-tech vehicles and mechanical bodies represent the essence of the futuristic metropolis. The set consists of several distinct locations, among which the old town and a 'special economic zone', Etoroff, are the most prominent. Oshii envisioned the set as being 'Chinese Gothic', combining ornamentation from the Eastern and Western cultural hemispheres. Etoroff derives its name from the largest of the South Kuril Islands, which were Japanese territory until the end of the Second World War. Although it is presently controlled by Russia, Japan also claims the island.

Innocence is a hybrid production that seamlessly combines 2DCG and 3DCG animation techniques. Oshii has said that the artwork for this project is unique, and is perhaps the star of the film. He believed the urban scenery should not be 'just something to fill the space behind the characters', stating that the 'silent world behind the characters is where the director has to communicate his core vision. The backgrounds are the director's vision of reality. There has to be something behind the characters that conveys a message.' As Oshii is not an animator, it was the artwork that provided the opportunity to make his mark (Oshii 2004b, p. 119). These ambitions resulted in extended shots of the city, especially of the Etoroff location.

For the film's art director Shuichi Kusamori, this was his first opportunity to work with Oshii directly. Previously, he had worked under the art direction of Hiromasa Ogura when drawing background artwork for both Patlabor movies and for *Ghost in*

Innocence, scene 2
Image board, *detail*
Shuichi Kusamori
Poster colour on paper
25 × 37 cm (9⅞ × 14⅝ in.)

Innocence starts, like *Ghost in the Shell*, in the old town. This part of the set was re-envisioned for *Innocence* to have the feel of a Chinatown district in an American city. It was further accentuated with elements from Taiwan and Hong Kong.

This image board from an early phase of the production conveys the mood of a hot, humid night, with careful attention to such details as the hues of buildings and the bill posters peeling off the walls (Oshii, 2004b, p. 68).

the Shell. While working on *Metropolis* (2001), Kusamori developed the skills in the digital domain for which he has since received acclaim. He is known in particular for his extremely detailed renderings of the surfaces of walls, and of signs of decay. In conversation with the author, he described himself as an illustrator who is usually doing 'too much' – he likes to add a lot of detail to his work, sometimes even to the point where the picture seems to be overloaded. This is in stark contrast to the style employed by Ogura, who prefers a more simple, 'cool' approach to his assignments. For Oshii's vision of a 'Chinese Gothic' style, rich in detail and ornamentation, Kusamori was the perfect choice as art director.

Innocence was a milestone in the digital transformation of the animation process. Oshii took the opportunity to explore the full potential of the art department, encouraging his staff to rethink and redesign the role of the art director (Oshii 2004b, p. 118). The nature of cel animation restricts the processes that a single artist can control. Digital production tools give each artist the ability to tackle far more, thus the various tasks can no longer be allocated so cleanly to individual creators. The boundaries between the role of the art director and colleagues in the artwork team often blur. In addition, Oshii introduced production designer Yohei Taneda, who usually works on live-action movies, to the team. This unusual step helped to further stimulate discussion among the outstanding creative personnel that he had assembled. Oshii has stated that, with this 'dream team', it was 'like being coach of Brazil's national soccer team. All the players are soccer artists' (Oshii 2004b, p. 119).

The effort and expense show, and the film has done much to burnish anime's reputation for high-quality artwork. In 2005, *Innocence* was the first anime film to be nominated for the Palme d'Or at the Cannes Film Festival.

Innocence, scene 33
Concept design
Takashi Watabe
Pencil on paper
17.6 × 25 cm (7 × 9⅞ in.)

Takashi Watabe served as the supervising layout artist on the production of *Innocence*. Together with art director Shuichi Kusamori and production designer Yohei Taneda, he created the set design for the film. Watabe developed the appearance of Etoroff, which resembles a forest of industrial towers.

Innocence, scene 33, cut no. 8
Image board
Shuichi Kusamori
Digital illustration

The city is wrapped in a haze of amber, almost as if it is breathing rust. This lighting effect embodies the theme of Etoroff as a 'city of iron, rust and glass'. The looming silhouettes of the structures and the detailing on their pinnacles combine to convey an urban landscape packed with buildings. A digital editing system (Quantel Domino) was used to add gas effects to the final image (Oshii 2004b, p. 9).

The opening sequence of Ridley Scott's *Blade Runner* (1982) presents a similar dystopian cityscape that finds a direct echo in the depiction of Etoroff. The earlier film's amber lighting was intensified for *Innocence*, and this may have inspired the sequel *Blade Runner 2049* (2017), directed by Denis Villeneuve, in turn.

Innocence, scene 33, cut no. 12
Image board
Shuichi Kusamori
Digital illustration

An image board of the headquarters of Locus Solus, a cyborg-manufacturing company. Takashi Watabe developed the concept design for this building and tried to express Mamoru Oshii's idea of a 'Chinese Gothic' architectural style. A repeating design element employed to achieve this look is the octagon – octagonal ornamentation appears not only in Etoroff's architecture but also on many other surfaces throughout the film's set. Fine detail underscores the scale of the building. The tips of the steeples are veiled in the ever-present haze.

Innocence, scene 33, cut no. 1
Image board
Shuichi Kusamori
Digital illustration

The bird's-eye view of this image board conveys a sense of Etoroff's fast-growing economy. A forest of skyscrapers spreads out concentrically from the city centre. The overall art concept for Etoroff was the 'white night of the far North'. Scenes take place at different times of day, each of which has its own character, but all are wrapped in a misty haze of amber lighting (Oshii 2004b, p. 6).

Innocence, scene 33, cut no. 19
Image board
Shuichi Kusamori
Poster colour on paper
28 × 38 cm (11⅛ × 15 in.)

This is the original paper-based artwork which Kusamori used to create the digital illustration.

Innocence, scene 33, cut no. 19
Image board
Shuichi Kusamori
Digital illustration

The image board for the tilt-rotor landing scene, looking directly down on the helipad, with its finely detailed feng shui compass. This compass was a last-minute idea, added just before completion. To convey the height of the landing pad, clouds are depicted moving in the air currents (Oshii 2004b, p. 15).

Innocence, scene 36, cut no. 4
Still image

Innocence, scene 36, cut no. 4
Image board
Shuichi Kusamori
Digital illustration

A gigantic, moving elephant sculpture mounted on a float participates in a festive parade through the city. This scene marks the midpoint of the story, and it occurs exactly halfway through the film's running time. Batou and Togusa, the main protagonists, are about to enter another dimension. The festival sequence has a similar dramaturgic function as corresponding sequences in the Patlabor movies (see p. 74) and *Ghost in the Shell* (see p. 94). While earlier sequences in *Innocence* have a more meditative feel, the festival sequence is an audiovisual celebration – it seems to act as an opportunity for the artwork team to celebrate its own capabilities.

The staff consulted numerous photos of Chinese festivals, which provided a useful guide to colour schemes. With the rust-coloured city acting as the backdrop, the use of red accents would not normally be effective – making them work was one of the many complex challenges that the artwork team set itself.

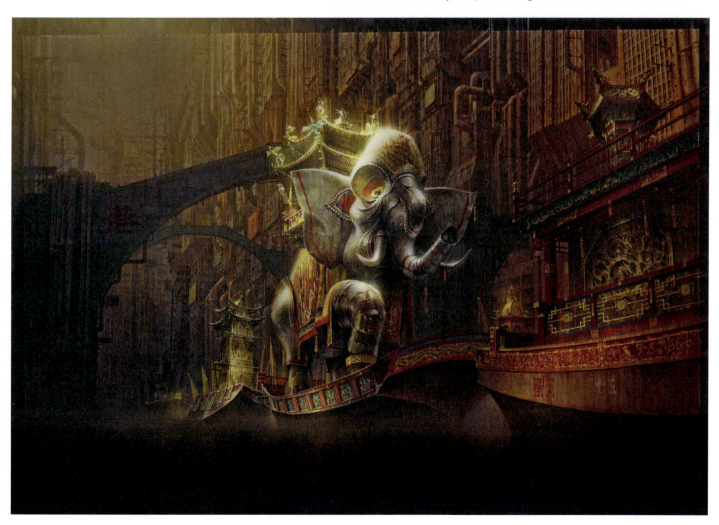

Innocence, scene 36, cut no. 29
Image board
Shuichi Kusamori
Poster colour on paper
24 × 36 cm (9½ × 14¼ in.)

Image board of one of the city's once-proud aqueducts, now nearly empty and fallen into disrepair. Following Oshii's requirements, the aqueducts are depicted as iron structures rather than being built in concrete and stone, as would usually be the case (Oshii 2004b, p. 18).

Innocence, scene 36, cut no. 29
Image board
Shuichi Kusamori
Digital illustration

Additional detail was then added, for instance the Chinese characters and the bill posters that are now pasted on the walls. Finally, the lighting was adjusted to achieve consistency with the film's overall amber lighting theme.

Innocence, scene 36, cut no. 38
Image board
Shuichi Kusamori
Digital illustration

Different lighting in the foreground and the background brings out the materiality of the ivory. In the background, upper areas are lit and lower sections lie in shadow. This approach is reversed in the foreground, creating a mysterious atmosphere (Oshii 2004b, p. 21).

Innocence, scene 36, cut no. 38
Image board
Shuichi Kusamori
Poster colour on paper
24 × 36 cm (9½ × 14¼ in.)

An image board of the deserted ruins of a temple with ivory walls. The team tried many different approaches to depict the appearance of ivory. The only non-ivory object is the copper relic in the centre of the frame, which provides a dark green accent to the composition.

Innocence, scene 15
Image board
Shuichi Kusamori
Poster colour on paper
24 × 37 cm (9½ × 14⅝ in.)

In line with the approach used elsewhere for the old city, the overall orange quality of the light alternates with occasional blue illuminations. Moist-looking wall surfaces with bills peeling off convey the sense of heat and humidity.

Innocence, scene 15
Image board
Shuichi Kusamori
Digital illustration

The lettering was changed in the digital version.

Innocence, scene 3
Image board
Shuichi Kusamori
Digital illustration

The alley is shown almost entirely from the protagonist's point of view, thus the backgrounds take the starring role. Extreme detailing was used, especially on pipes, wall surfaces and tiles (Oshii 2004b, p. 73).

Innocence, scene 23
Image board
Shuichi Kusamori
Digital illustration

This hand-drawn artwork depicting the old town was used in two digital renderings as a day view and as a night view. In the end, only the daylight view made it into the production background.

Innocence, scene 23
Image board
Shuichi Kusamori
Digital illustration

Innocence, scene 24
Image board
Shuichi Kusamori
Poster colour on paper
23 × 36 cm (9⅛ × 14¼ in.)

Image board of the headquarters of a criminal gang. In the final production background, Chinese characters by the calligrapher Lai Wai were added. This action sequence uses cel animation, while its backgrounds adhere to traditional anime conventions, thus are the most orthodox in the film (Oshii 2004b, p. 94).

Innocence, scene 24
Image board
Shuichi Kusamori
Digital illustration

Innocence, scene 24
Still image

Innocence, scene 56, cut no. 8
Concept design
Takashi Watabe
Pencil on paper
17.6 × 25 cm (7 × 9⅞ in.)

As supervising layout artist, Takashi Watabe developed concept designs and layouts. The following drawings depict the inside of a cyborg-production facility, which is located on the ship that provides the location for the final showdown. To create this plant ship, Oshii drew on his experience animating a similar facility, the 'ark' in *Patlabor 2: The Movie* (1993).

Although these drawings were intended as concept designs, some of them acted more as layouts for the film. In addition, because of the lighting, most of the details can hardly be seen in the final images and were not modelled in the digital domain. These renderings in pencil on paper give an insight into a part of the diegetic world that is only visible at this stage of the production process.

Innocence, scene 59a, cut no. 1
Concept design
Takashi Watabe
Pencil on paper
17.6 × 25 cm (7 × 9⅞ in.)

Watabe's annotations on the drawing specify that the floor of the walkway should be a grating, and that there should be a handrail on the right-hand side of the walkway.

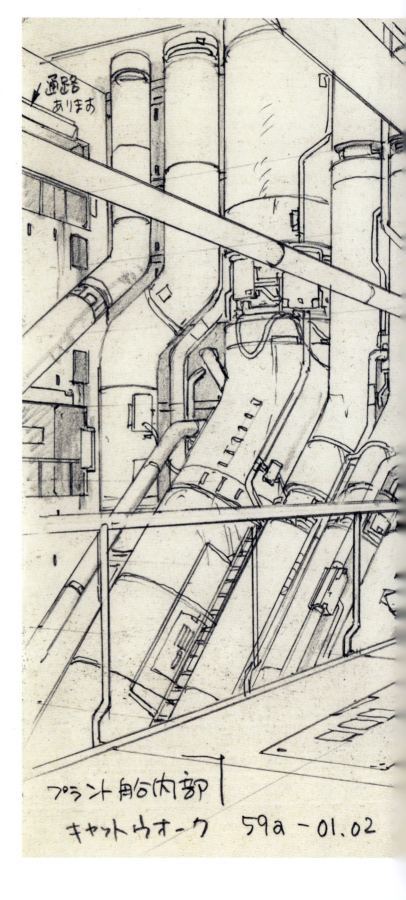

Innocence, scene 59a, cut no. 1
Still image

Innocence, scene 59, cut no. 5
Still image

Innocence, scene 59, cut no. 5
Concept design
Takashi Watabe
Pencil on paper
17.6 × 25 cm (7 × 9⅞ in.)

View from the top looking down onto the walkway. Watabe's care in depicting the intricate cables and pipelines reflects the factory's status as the 'nerve centre' of the film, as well as the film's overall theme of interconnected networks.

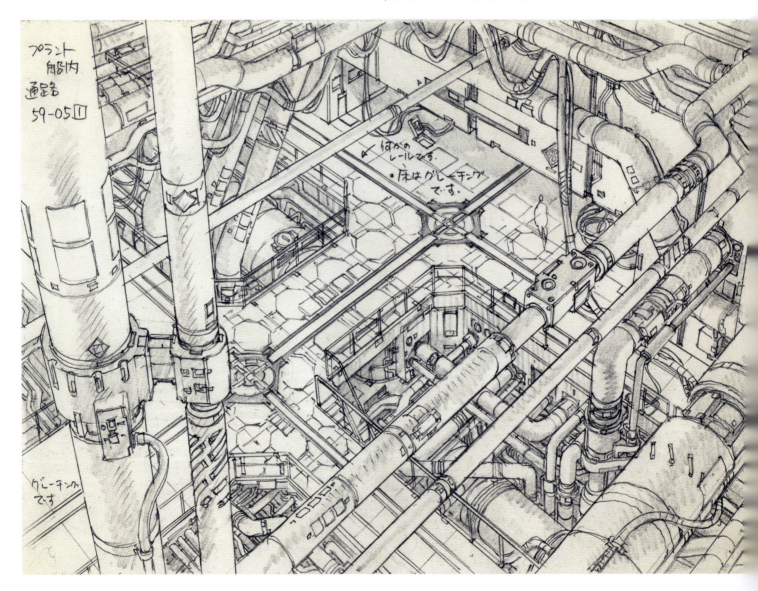

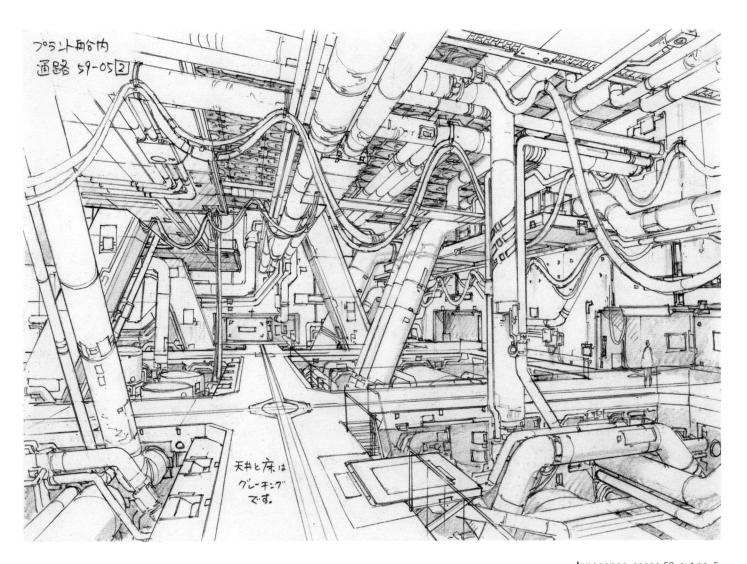

Innocence, scene 59, cut no. 5
Concept design
Takashi Watabe
Pencil on paper
17.6 × 25 cm (7 × 9⅞ in.)

View from the walkway.

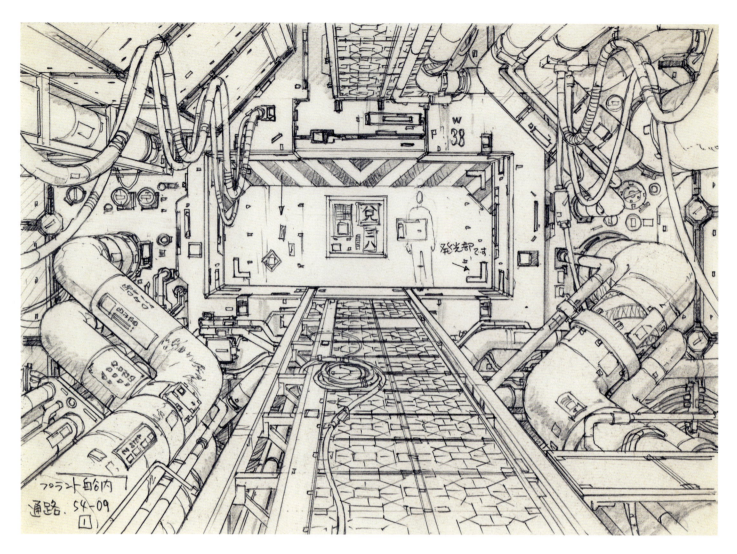

Innocence, scene 54, cut no. 9
Concept design
Takashi Watabe
Pencil on paper
17.6 × 25 cm (7 × 9⅞ in.)

The approach to a sliding door. The floor is designed with a grating similar in scale to those appearing in other interiors in the film. The ornamentation draws on the octagonal theme that crops up throughout the production design. However, as on many other occasions, the final screen image is too dark to see these meticulous details.

Innocence, scene 54, cut no. 9
Still image

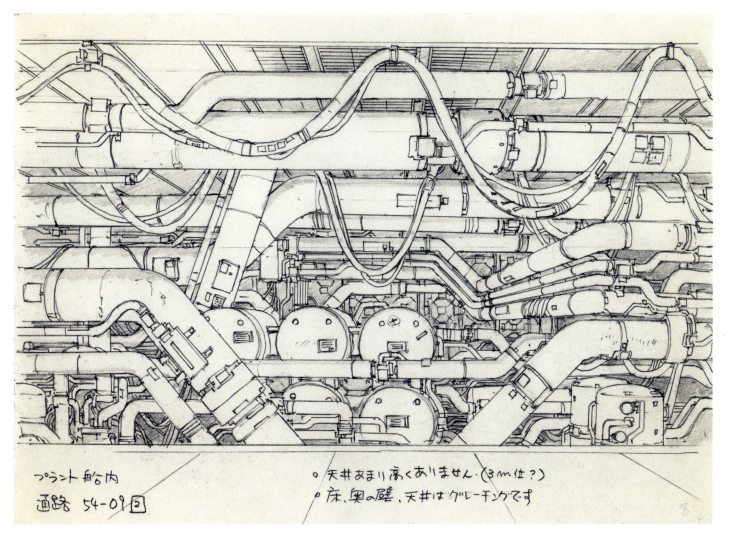

Innocence, scene 54, cut no. 9
Concept design
Takashi Watabe
Pencil on paper
17.6 × 25 cm (7 × 9⅞ in.)

The door slides open and reveals more pipes and cables in the hallway behind. The comments specify that the ceiling is quite low, at approximately three metres.

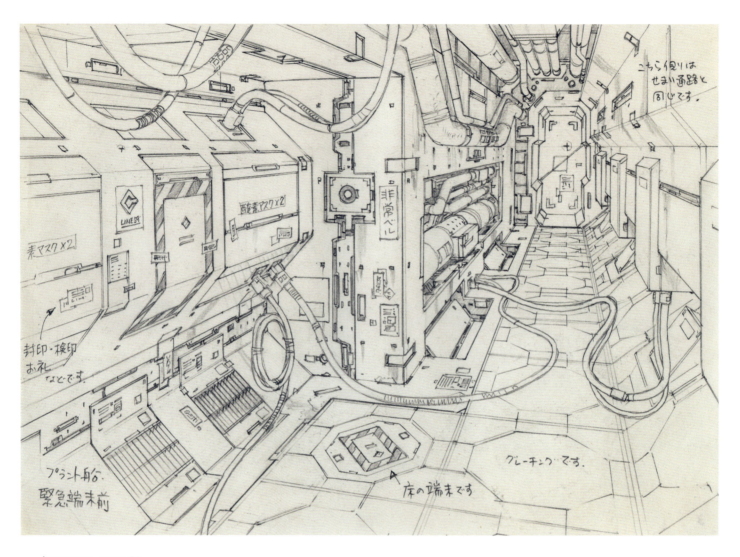

Innocence, scene 54
Concept design
Takashi Watabe
Pencil on paper
17.6 × 25 cm (7 × 9⅞ in.)

Watabe always elaborates his concept designs in detail and explains the functions of the mechanical and technical elements he has devised. In this design, he illustrates the functioning and use of a deadbolt in the interior of the factory ship.

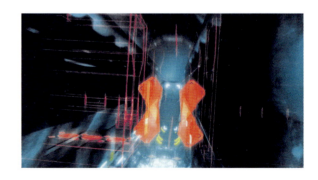

Innocence, scene 54, cut no. 6
Still image

182   Innocence

Innocence, scene 54
Concept design
Takashi Watabe
Pencil on paper
17.6 × 25 cm (7 × 9⅞ in.)

This concept design explains how to open the door, and also shows how the two panels that are revealed during this process are detailed with a convexo-concave structure that correlates with the grating of the floor.

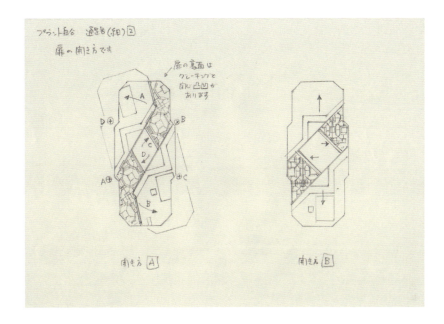

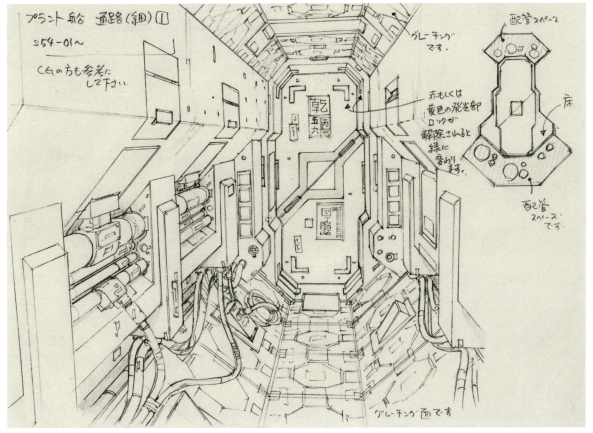

Innocence, scene 54
Concept design
Takashi Watabe
Pencil on paper
17.6 × 25 cm (7 × 9⅞ in.)

This close-up of the space depicted in the concept design opposite specifies the door's functioning. Red or yellow lights are to be used, which turn green when it is unlocked. A diagram on the upper right shows artworkers that there are pipes that are not currently visible running above and below the door. Watabe also writes that this drawing should be shown to those working on the digital animation of the door.

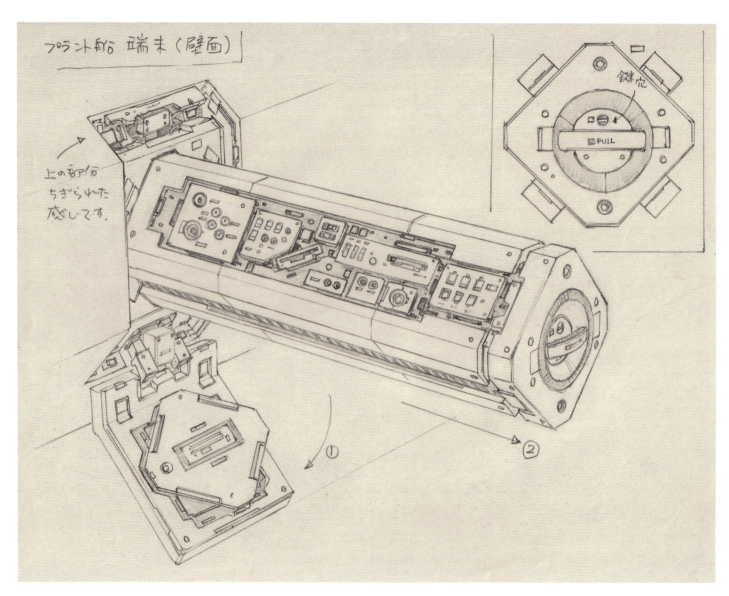

Innocence, scene 54
Concept design
Takashi Watabe
Pencil on paper
17.6 × 25 cm (7 × 9⅞ in.)

Innocence, scene 54
Concept design
Takashi Watabe
Pencil on paper
17.6 × 25 cm (7 × 9⅞ in.)

The comments on this concept design specify that the lid opens after gliding upwards for about ten centimetres. Once the cover has opened, the plug device rises up as well.

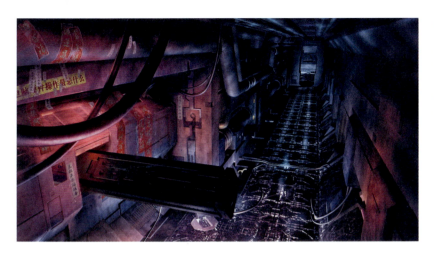

Innocence, scene 54
Image board
Shuichi Kusamori
Digital illustration

Kusamori based this digital illustration directly on Watabe's concept designs.

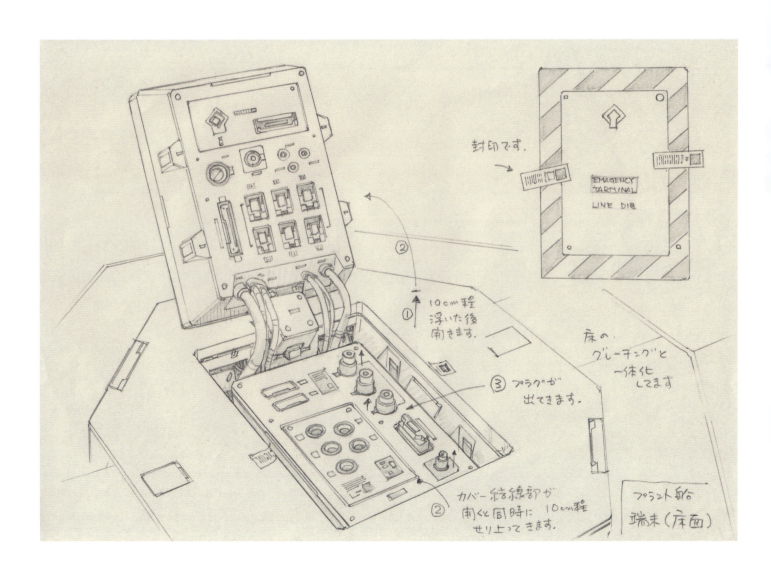

TEKKONKINKREET

The urban fabric in *Tekkonkinkreet*, with its rambling wooden structures, busy covered markets and labyrinthine corridors, is a homage to the fast-disappearing architecture of Showa-era Tokyo, and a study in the relationship between nostalgia and modernity, hope and regret.

Tekkonkinkreet, 2006. DIR.: **Michael Arias.** SCR.: **Anthony Weintraub.** ART: **Shinji Kimura.** ANI.: **Shojiro Nishimi.** MUS.: **Plaid.** PRD.: **Studio 4°C, Aniplex. 110 mins.**

Based on Taiyo Matsumoto's manga of the same name, originally serialized from 1993 to 1994, *Tekkonkinkreet* tells the story of two young street kids, Black and White, in a city nicknamed Takaramachi – Treasure Town. The film's title refers to a child's mispronunciation of steel-reinforced concrete (*tekkin konkurito*). The arrival of a Yakuza boss, Snake, and his mob changes Black and White's lives. The gangsters want to renovate the neighbourhood with new buildings and build a huge amusement park, Kiddie Kastle.

Tekkonkinkreet was produced by Studio 4°C, whose productions include the three-part film *Memories by Katsuhiro Otomo* (1995), overseen by the director of *AKIRA* (1988), and several episodes from a short-film series produced by the Wachowskis, *The Animatrix* (2003). Studio 4°C's works all feature a very distinctive style, which is also evident in *Tekkonkinkreet*. This consistency is in large part the achievement of the studio's founder, the producer Eiko Tanaka.

Tekkonkinkreet was the directorial debut of Los Angeles-born Michael Arias, who became famous in the animation industry as the inventor of 'toon-shading' algorithms. With his software, it became possible to render computer-generated animation in a way that makes it appear as if it were cel animation. *Tekkonkinkreet* is a hybrid of traditional and digital animation, although it was originally planned as a completely computer-animated project. The finished production uses computer animation in only forty per cent of its scenes – most of the animation work was done on paper. Arias decided that he wanted to focus on directing, not on computer animation or software. At Studio 4°C, he found himself surrounded by a group of drafters that he considered 'to be the best character animators in the world' and he wanted them to work with tools that they knew well, that is with pencil and paper. Furthermore, Arias believed that hand-drawn artistic representations of the characters were more expressive than 3D animation (Kimura 2006a, p. 256).

Treasure Town's visuals are in line with the original manga, although the city did not feature as prominently in the manga as it does in the anime. The development and elaboration of Treasure Town were in large part the achievement of art director Shinji Kimura. Before working on *Tekkonkinkreet*, Kimura had served as an art director on

Tekkonkinkreet
Image board, *detail*
Shinji Kimura
Poster colour on paper
20 × 38 cm (7⅞ × 15 in.)

'How would children of Black and White's age draw clouds at night?' It was this question that sparked Shinji Kimura's imagination and inspired him to create this image board (Kimura, personal interview, 2019).

Kimura drew just a few image boards for the project because he felt comfortable relying on the skills of his staff once he had laid out his basic ideas. Only key images, such as this night-view overlooking Treasure Town, one of Black and White's house, and another depicting the colours around the train station (see p. 189) were drawn by him.

Katsuhiro Otomo's *Steamboy* (2004). He depicts Treasure Town as a theme park from the early Showa era (1926–89), with wooden houses, cavernous corridors, covered markets and garish billboards. Its streets burst with life and endless traffic. Instead of casting the city in neon lights and gloom in a *Blade Runner*-like fashion, the artists at Studio 4°C found much of their inspiration on the doorstep. A warren of corridors in the market area of Kichijoji, the town in which Studio 4°C is based, provided the basis for their vision of Treasure Town's urban fabric.

Arias regards *Tekkonkinkreet* as a study of contrasts: good and evil, light and shadow, creation and destruction, love and hate, innocence and guilt, nostalgia and modernity, hope and regret. While the contrasts are implicit in the story, Arias also hoped to create explicit references to them through the film's visuals (Arias 2004). Seen through Black and White's eyes, the city is at times a rosy-coloured playground, at other times a shadowy labyrinth. Arias drew elements from the fantastic streets in Marc Caro and Jean-Pierre Jeunet's *The City Of Lost Children* (1995) and the earthbound slum in Akira Kurosawa's *Dodes'ka-den* (1970). But, as with both of those imaginary cities, Arias wanted Treasure Town to be 'entirely believable in its unreality'. He conceived of Treasure Town as a living organism, with Black as its soul, and White as its conscience. He wanted the antiquated Treasure Town to exert a warm nostalgic pull on viewers, helping them to truly sympathize with the boys' dread as Snake's Kiddie Kastle casts its sinister shadow on the old shops and alleys (Arias 2004).

Instead of treating characters and backgrounds in a consistent manner from one shot to another, as in most anime, Arias opted to shift between contrasting animation styles that reflected the internal states of the characters: 'Daylight sequences that focus on Black and White's life on the Treasure Town streets will be shown as though shot by a child's instant camera, while scenes of Treasure Town nightlife will be shot in the neo-realistic documentary style typical of the photographs of Daido Moriyama or Nobuyoshi Araki' (Arias 2004).

Arias favoured 'a documentary-style handheld camera over the perfect compositions that anchor most traditional animation', and this improvisational camerawork served as his key expressive tool. Although extensive use of a handheld camera was both an artistic and a technical challenge, it was central to his directing strategy, and he regarded it as crucial to setting the production apart from other anime. The use of a handheld camera in animation requires a three-dimensional space, otherwise the viewpoint cannot move freely. As a result, there are few final production backgrounds among Shinji Kimura's work for *Tekkonkinkreet*. Most of his paper-based work was cut up digitally (and at times also physically) and then composited onto the 3D scenery of the shot. This combination of extremely condensed pseudo-3D backgrounds, yet with a great variety of detail in each setting, was unprecedented at the time of production.

Tekkonkinkreet
Image board
Shinji Kimura
Poster colour on paper
22.5 × 32 cm (8⅞ × 12⅝ in.)

Treasure Town train station in a rendering created early in the production process by Kimura.

Tekkonkinkreet, scene boards
Shinji Kimura
Poster colour on paper
Each 8 × 17 cm (3¼ × 6¾ in.)

Guided by Eiko Tanaka, the producer at Studio 4°C, Shinji Kimura drew these scene boards during the early stages of production. Kimura included the characters (a task usually undertaken by the animation director) to give a better impression of how the images might look like as the story unfolds. These boards were used to achieve a consistent look as more staff joined the team.

The protagonists, Black and White, move up and down structures with ease, therefore all locations are shown from contrasting perspectives, ranging from bird's-eye to ground-level views. Michael Arias wanted to exploit these vertical movements as a means to reinforce – and occasionally contradict – the ups and downs of the film's narrative (Kimura 2006b, p. 20).

Tekkonkinkreet
Production background
Shinji Kimura
Poster colour on paper
32 × 78 cm (12⅝ × 30¾ in.)

This large production background was used in the first scene and gives an overview of Treasure Town. Railway tracks and highways cross the old town, which is located on an eye-shaped island. The view is from a 'first-bird perspective', as seen by a crow that features prominently in the opening sequence. The final shot is warped digitally to increase the impression that it has been taken with a wide-angle lens.

Tekkonkinkreet
Art setting
Shinji Kimura
Pencil on paper
29.7 × 42 cm (11¾ × 16⅝ in.)

This overview of Treasure Town is based precisely on the city map (see pp. 198–99). Black and White live under the highway on the right side of the island, just opposite the factory.

宝町 全景

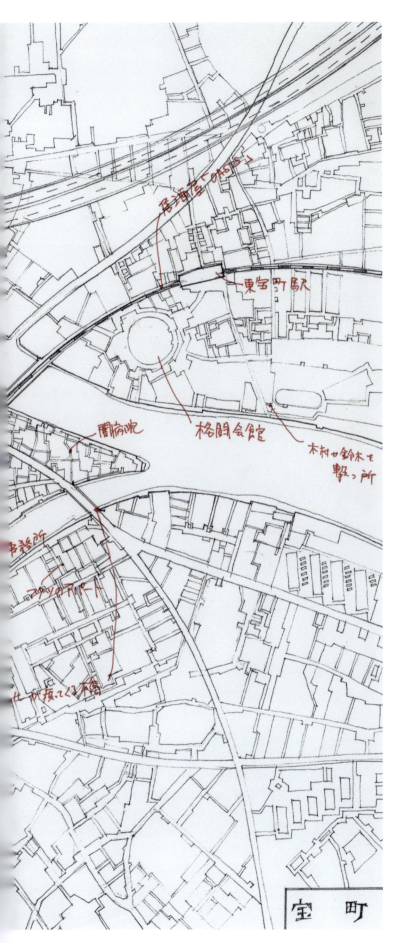

Tekkonkinkreet, city map
Shinji Kimura
Fine liner on photocopy
28 × 36 cm (11⅛ × 14¼ in.)

On this map of Treasure Town, Shinji Kimura has marked all the locations of the story. A coloured version of this drawing features as a background motif in several shots scattered throughout the film.

Tekkonkinkreet, Black and White's house, no. 1
Art setting
Shinji Kimura
Pencil on paper
21 × 30 cm (8⅜ × 11⅞ in.)

In Kimura's 'art settings', he gives several perspectives of a shot's location and conveys the atmosphere of the place. These drawings are rich in detail because subsequent production steps, including camerawork, had to be based on them.

Tekkonkinkreet, Black and White's house
Image board
Shinji Kimura
Poster colour on paper
20 × 37 cm (7⅞ × 14⅝ in.)

Black and White live under the highway, close to the riverside. The streak of light that hits the car is leaking from the slits in the bridge above.

Tekkonkinkreet, Black and White's house
Image board
Shinji Kimura
Poster colour on paper
20 × 37 cm (7⅞ × 14⅝ in.)

Tekkonkinkreet, Black and White's house, no. 2
Art setting
Shinji Kimura
Pencil on paper
21 × 30 cm (8⅜ × 11⅞ in.)

Tekkonkinkreet
Production background
Shinji Kimura
Poster colour on paper
29 × 38 cm (11½ × 15 in.)

As in *AKIRA* (1988), *Neon Genesis Evangelion* (1995), *Metropolis* (2001) and *Innocence* (2004), *Tekkonkinkreet* employs industrial piping as a prominent motif. This factory is located on the riverside, right opposite Black and White's home. Kimura wanted to have the entire screen buried under this immense structure, as if Black were looking at the dark side of the world (Kimura 2006a, p. 89).

Tekkonkinkreet, scene 3, cut no. 34
Still image

Tekkonkinkreet
Production background
Shinji Kimura
Poster colour on paper
25.5 × 36 cm (10⅛ × 14¼ in.)

Tekkonkinkreet, scene 7, cut no. 82
Still image

Tekkonkinkreet, alley
Art setting
Shinji Kimura
Pencil on paper
36 × 25.5 cm (14¼ × 10⅛ in.)

Tekkonkinkreet, alley
Image board
Shinji Kimura
Poster colour on paper
37.6 × 29 cm (14⅞ × 11½ in.)

Tekkonkinkreet, billboard
Art setting
Shinji Kimura
Pencil on paper
21 × 30 cm (8⅜ × 11⅞ in.)

Black and White perched on top of a billboard, with lettering that reads 'Transportation Society'. Kimura intended to have the two characters sitting on the side of the rotating wheel that slopes downwards, as here, as it felt scarier to him. However, in the final image the wheel is angled upwards, which gives the scene a more uplifting feel (Kimura 2006a, p. 26).

Tekkonkinkreet, scene 3, cut no. 19
Still image

Tekkonkinkreet, tramway
Art setting
Shinji Kimura
Pencil on paper
21 × 30 cm (8 3/8 × 11 7/8 in.)

The Metropolitan Electric Railway sneaks out of a narrow street. Kimura created this composition with the aim of giving the image greater depth. He also liked the idea of a cityscape so narrow and dense that accidents might occur at any moment, exacerbated by the complexity of the junction (Kimura 2006b, p. 85). The drawing is on the reverse side of a regular layout sheet belonging to Studio 4°C, and the studio's mark is visible in the top right corner, showing through the paper.

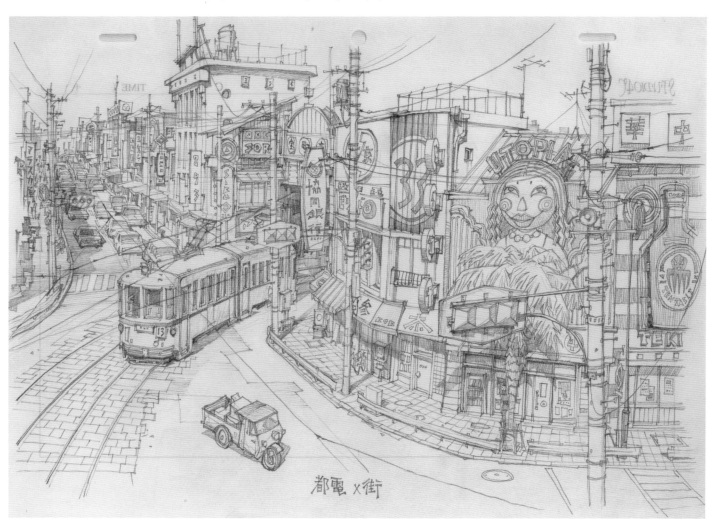

Tekkonkinkreet, Mimizuku Hospital
Art setting
Shinji Kimura
Pencil on paper
21 × 30 cm (8⅜ × 11⅞ in.)

A bird's-eye view of the Mimizuku Hospital as visualized in the initial scene board (see p. 192). Black stands on the electricity pole and observes the situation. Although Treasure Town's design breaks with almost all conventions of a post-*Blade Runner* dystopia, it cannot dispense with either poles or pipes.

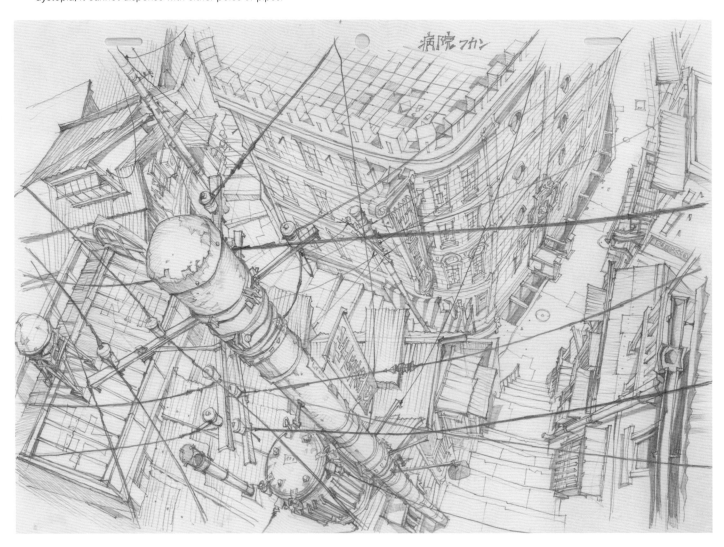

Tekkonkinkreet, Takara Shrine
Art setting
Shinji Kimura
Pencil on paper
21 × 30 cm (8⅜ × 11⅞ in.)

Although Treasure Town is a stateless free city, Kimura figured it would still be better not to break with convention in the depiction of this shrine. The scene bears a strong resemblance to Nakamise, a traditional Tokyo shopping street that runs in front of Sensoji Temple in Asakusa (Kimura 2006a, p. 165).

Tekkonkinkreet, Chuo Dori
Image board
Shinji Kimura
Poster colour on paper
25 × 53 cm (9⅞ × 20⅞ in.)

This is Treasure Town's main street, modelled after Ginza as it looked during the early Showa era. In the original manga by Taiyo Matsumoto, this cityscape is established by a single frame on one page, but Kimura expands and develops Matsumoto's vision significantly.

Tekkonkinkreet, park, lower stairs
Art setting
Shinji Kimura
Pencil on paper
21 × 30 cm (8 3/8 × 11 7/8 in.)

This art setting shows the approach to Octopus Hill Park from its lower stairs. The staircase at the very top reaches the park.

Tekkonkinkreet, scene 3, cut no. 56
Still image

Tekkonkinkreet, scene 7, cut no. 13
Still image

Tekkonkinkreet, park, overview
Art setting
Shinji Kimura
Pencil on paper
21 × 30 cm (8⅜ × 11⅞ in.)

Aerial view of Octopus Hill Park. The eponymous octopus sculpture is located in the middle of the playground area. The staircase shown in the previous art setting reaches the park at the bottom left. Straight ahead, on the left-hand side, is the bench that is depicted in great detail in the next two art settings (see pp. 214–15).

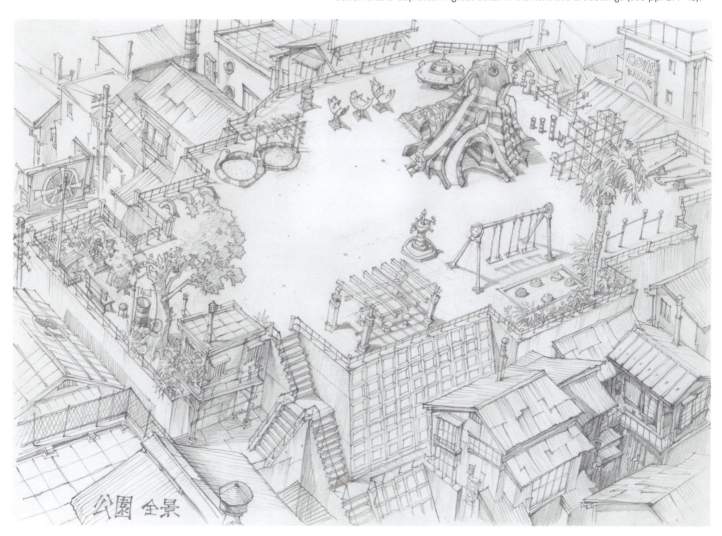

Tekkonkinkreet, park, no. 1
Art setting
Shinji Kimura
Pencil on paper
21 × 30 cm (8 3/8 × 11 7/8 in.)

This setting depicts the top of the stairs that lead to Octopus Hill Park. Treasure Town has little greenery, except in this one planted area. This is the home of Gramps, an outsider like Black and White and their true friend. Kimura drew on Mahatma Gandhi's life when imagining a spiritual existence for this character. Gramps lives inside a fence that is entirely surrounded by the city.

Tekkonkinkreet, park, no. 2
Art setting
Shinji Kimura
Pencil on paper
21 × 30 cm (8⅜ × 11⅞ in.)

Tekkonkinkreet
Production background
Shinji Kimura
Poster colour on paper
25.5 × 36 cm (10⅛ × 14¼ in.)

A production background showing Gramps's bench in the public park. This is his place to meditate on the city and on life, and give occasional advice to Black and White.

Tekkonkinkreet, scene 3, cut no. 62
Still image

White approaches Gramps, then sits next to him.

Tekkonkinkreet, scene 3, cut no. 98
Still image

Tekkonkinkreet, public bath
Art setting
Shinji Kimura
Pencil on paper
21 × 30 cm (8⅜ × 11⅞ in.)

Kimura designed the tiles in this setting to make the public bath look as if it dates back to the old days. One of Kimura's specialities is the depiction of weathered surfaces and signs of decay. Similarly, the mural in the background showing Mount Fuji appears to be on the verge of falling down. The final production background was drawn by Akemi Konno (Kimura 2006a, p. 81).

Tekkonkinkreet, scene 2, cut no. 116
Still image

Gramps taking a shower with Black and White in the public bath.

Tekkonkinkreet, public bath
Production background
Shinji Kimura
Poster colour on paper
25.5 × 36 cm (10⅛ × 14¼ in.)

Public baths like this can still be found occasionally in the older, eastern parts of Tokyo.

Tekkonkinkreet, scene 2, cut no. 112
Still image

Tekkonkinkreet
Production background
Shinji Kimura
Poster colour on paper
25.5 × 36 cm (10⅛ × 14¼ in.)

The opening image for the last chapter of the film. In this section, the Kiddie Castle, here illuminated as the focus of attention, is destroyed and peace in Treasure Town is restored. Right next to the highway, a billboard advertises '109', a reference to a popular department store in Shibuya that has a target audience of teenagers just a little older than Black and White.

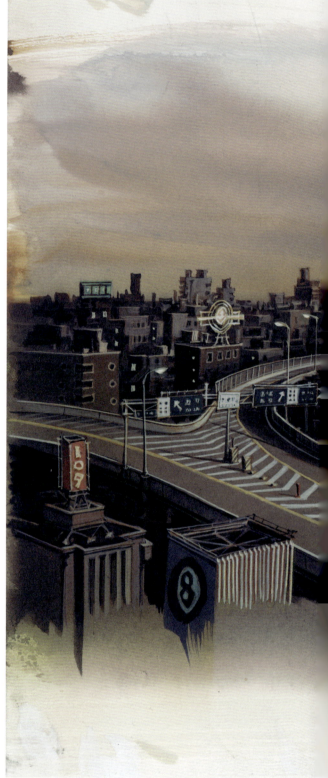

Tekkonkinkreet, Kiddie Kastle
Production background
Shinji Kimura
Poster colour on paper
24.5 × 43 cm (9¾ × 17 in.)

Kiddie Kastle at night – the central tower is inspired by the photographic work of the German artists Bernd and Hilla Becher (Kimura 2006b, p. 90).

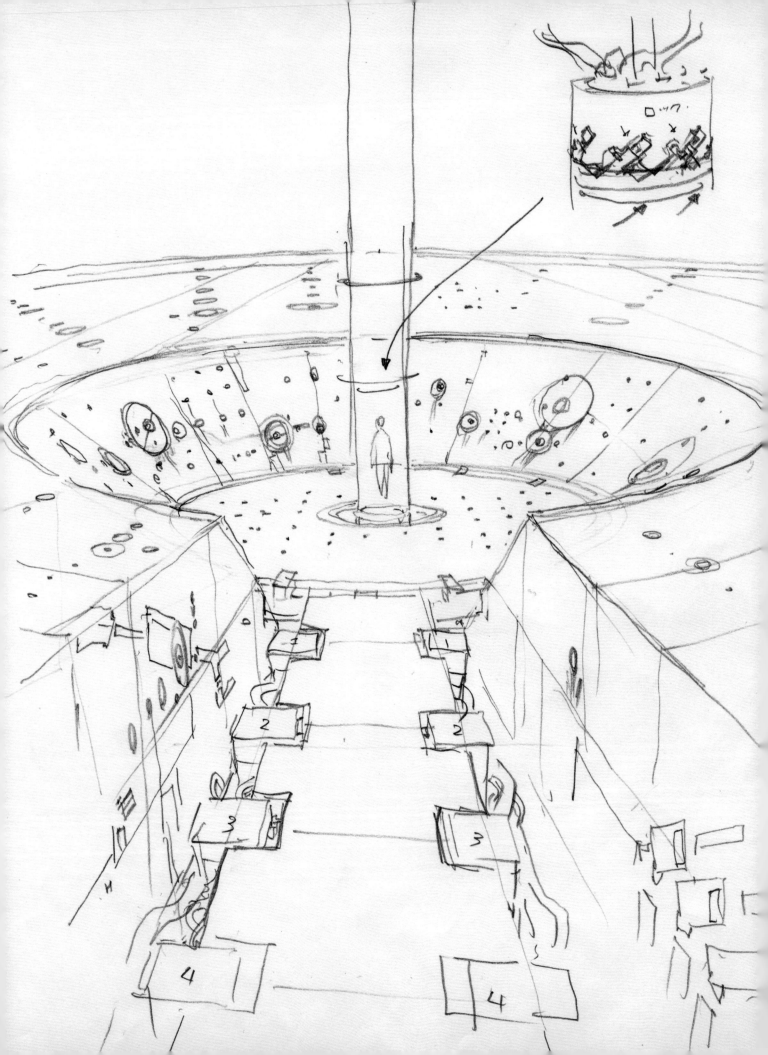

REBUILD OF EVANGELION

Hideaki Anno's *Neon Genesis Evangelion* series is one of the most important franchises in anime, focusing on Tokyo-3, a vast fortress city that is both organic and artificial. Its intricate, evolving infrastructure infuses this urban battleground with a unique aesthetic vision.

Neon Genesis Evangelion, 1995 (TV); 2007, 2009 (Rebuild of Evangelion movies). DIR.: Hideaki Anno, Kazuya Tsurumaki. SCR.: Hideaki Anno, Akio Satsugawa. DES.: Yoshiyuki Sadamoto, Ikuto Yamashita. ANI.: Kazuya Tsurumaki, Tadashi Hiramatsu. MUS.: Shiro Sagisu. PRD.: Tatsunoko, Gainax, TV Tokyo (TV); Studio Khara (movies). 25 mins × 26 episodes (TV); 101 mins (Evangelion: 1.0 You Are [Not] Alone); 108 mins (Evangelion: 2.0 You Can [Not] Advance).

Neon Genesis Evangelion (1995) was originally a twenty-six-part series, broadcast weekly on Japanese television between October 1995 and March 1996. The series introduced the medium of anime to new audiences, both in Japan and abroad. It subsequently formed the basis of several films, manga and video games, and is regarded as one of the most important anime franchises.

The story of *Neon Genesis Evangelion* is set in the near future, as seen from the 1990s. In the year 2000 a cataclysmic explosion, called Second Impact, is caused by a 'contact experiment' with a humanoid creature that has been discovered buried in the Antarctic. Three billion people die as a result. The creature was the first Angel, an alien force that threatens humanity. The secret organization NERV is founded to protect humanity from further devastating Impacts. NERV's headquarters is set up in a huge underground cavern, on the surface of which lies the fortress city Tokyo-3. NERV develops the Evangelions that give the franchise its name – giant humanoid robots, controlled by specially qualified teenagers, the Children. As more and more Angels approach Earth (Japan), the Evangelions are humanity's last line of defence.

Hideaki Anno, who created and directed the series, is particularly dedicated to the realistic representation of Tokyo-3, which provides the central location for the entire franchise. The city serves as a bastion against attacks by the Angels, and is situated on the northern shore of Lake Ashi in Hakone. At first glance it seems prosaic, combining elements of a small Japanese town with the metropolis of Tokyo. But, beneath its tranquil surface, Tokyo-3 is a vast machine that can change within minutes into a fortress equipped for battle. For protection against Angel attacks, most of the city's buildings are capable of being retracted beneath the surface. The Evangelion Units are launched from under the city using access gates disguised as buildings. Tokyo-3 is a machine that only pretends to be alive – its sole purpose is to serve as a battlefield.

Anno shares the fascination for urban infrastructures – the nerve centres of the modern city – evident in the work of Katsuhiro Otomo and Mamoru Oshii. However,

Evangelion: 2.0, cut no. 710
Rough sketch, *detail*
Takashi Watabe
Pencil and printout on paper
17.6 × 25 cm (7 × 9⅞ in.)

unlike many in the science-fiction genre, he has little apparent interest in imposing cyberpunk stylings on cityscapes. While Otomo develops his vision through the process of drawing and Oshii creates imagery 'as if it were live action', Anno's designs are influenced by another medium, taking the miniature sets of tokusatsu films as their starting point. Tokusatsu – literally 'special effects' – is a popular genre of Japanese TV and film culture. The term refers to the mechanical and optical effects used on set during shooting, in contrast to 'visual effects', which are applied in post-production. Tokusatsu is used as a generic description for live-action films with stories that revolve around a series of special-effects shots. The best-known Japanese examples are monster films such as Godzilla (1954), directed by Ishiro Honda, and the superhero TV series Ultraman (1966–67), directed by Hajime Tsuburaya and Akio Jissoji.

A typical tokusatsu scenario has three elements: one or more aggressors; a city that acts as a battleground; and a defending superhero. An important factor is the relative sizes of the protagonists and the set. Monsters and superheroes are usually portrayed as giants, and are played by actors in costume and prosthetics; the set is constructed in miniature, and forms the arena for the battle between good and evil. For fight scenes, the set is often arranged in a ring around the characters. The protagonists then trample down large parts, effectively razing sections of the city to the ground.

Tokusatsu director Eiji Tsuburaya was a pioneer in the genre, working with specialists from the model-railway industry to produce ever more perfect miniature sets. He developed the special effects for both Godzilla and Ultraman, and his models were renowned for being visually compact and realistic on screen. Hideaki Anno's work repeatedly draws on Tsuburaya's innovations, and Ultraman seems to have had a particular influence on the conception of Neon Genesis Evangelion – as a student, Anno even created a tribute film called Return of Ultraman in 1983, taking the role of the hero himself.

In Neon Genesis Evangelion, the depiction of the heroes (the Children) in their huge Evangelions battling the monsters (the Angels) within the urban setting of Tokyo-3 is a direct reference to this tokusatsu formula, transformed into the medium of anime. Anno admires tokusatsu for its specific aesthetic qualities and, for him, its films have an affinity with anime in the sense that both are created 'by hand'. Furthermore, 'a certain kind of energy emerges when things are compressed and made into miniatures. In the process of making it smaller, the feelings of the creators are poured into it. This is the main point of miniature sets.' As a result, Anno is 'more impressed by a miniature that looks exactly like a real scene than by the real scene itself' (Anno 2008, p. 452). He draws his layouts with the idea of tokusatsu in mind – his closest partner in the creation of sets is not the art director but his special-effects expert, Shinji Higuchi.

In Anno's radical perspective, the city appears as the sum total of all available technologies. As the ultimate extension of human senses and organs, it is both artificial and organic, thus Tokyo-3 is itself a cyborg. The layouts presented here were created for the Rebuild of Evangelion feature-length films, remaking the original TV series of 1995. Sadly, most of the drawings for that first TV series have been lost or have deteriorated, but these new layouts were all created by Anno himself, so are well suited to convey the architectural vision of his work. These layouts present the last step in the production process that still involves drawing with pencil on paper – all subsequent steps are executed digitally. Therefore, some areas may be void of any information, just specifying that the part in question will later be drawn in 3DCG.

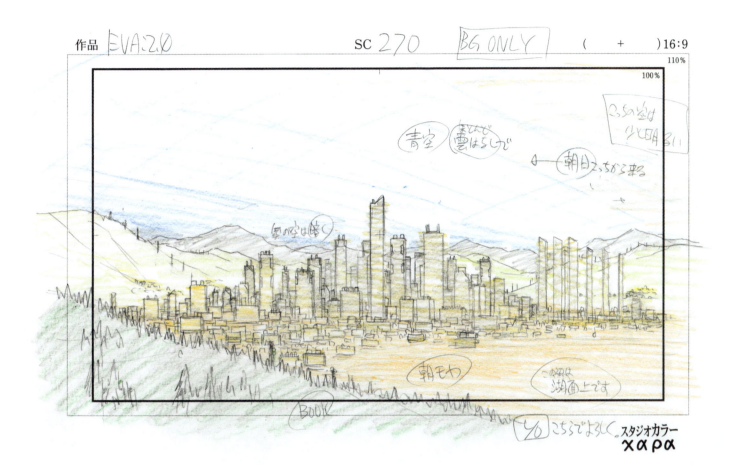

Evangelion: 2.0, cut no. 270
Layout
Hideaki Anno
Pencil on paper
26 × 37 cm (10¼ × 14⅝ in.)

Tokyo-3 lies dormant. The city is supposed to be located just north of Lake Ashi in the Hakone area, a popular holiday resort for Tokyo residents. The layout specifies this cut as 'BG only' – background only – which means that no animated characters are to be added to the shot.

Evangelion: 2.0, cut no. 270
Still image

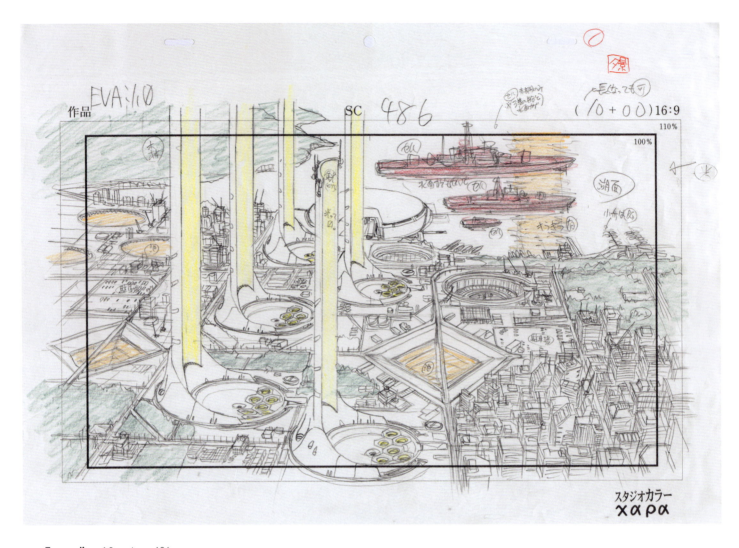

Evangelion: 1.0, cut no. 486
Layout
Hideaki Anno
Pencil on paper
26 × 37 cm (10¼ × 14⅝ in.)

Massive solar-energy collection blocks are erected in the waterfront district at the southern end of Tokyo-3, providing light and electrical power for the city. The warships in the background of this layout are a motif that features prominently throughout the series. All the characters are named after warships from the Imperial Japanese Navy during the Second World War.

Evangelion: 1.0, cut no. 486
Still image

Photo archive
Digital photography, 2006–08
Hideaki Anno

Anno is a passionate photographer of electricity pylons, cables and construction sites. Unlike those of Haruhiko Higami and others, these photographs are not taken as part of a location-hunting process – they do not present certain camera angles or final perspectives. Anno takes these pictures for the details, guided by such questions as: 'What does the power pylon really look like?' For him, it is important to gather as much detail as possible of such intricate urban infrastructures to infuse his works with realism. His method implies a certain kind of fetishism for technical detail (Anno 2010, p. 352). He has a very large collection of photos that he uses as a source of inspiration – only a small selection is presented here.

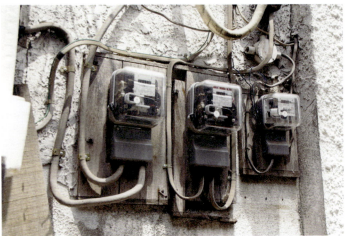

Evangelion: 1.0, cut no. 488
Layout
Hideaki Anno
Pencil on paper
26 × 37 cm (10¼ × 14⅝ in.)

Tokyo-3 was conceived as a bastion against the enemy attackers. If the city has to be defended, the inhabited buildings are sunk underground and replaced with military structures such as missile catapults and gun turrets. The idea was borrowed from the British TV series *Stingray* (1964–65) created by Gerry and Sylvia Anderson for ITC Entertainment (Anno 2008, p. 453).

In his designs for Tokyo-3, Anno makes use of contour lines with reduced tonal values, an approach that is usually reserved for the characters in anime films, thus the status of this transformable machine city is raised to match those of the story's living protagonists. This layout by Anno specifies the speed of the buildings' movement.

Evangelion: 1.0, cut no. 488
Still image

Tokyo-3 emerging from its underground battle formation to its full elevation.

230 Rebuild of Evangelion

Evangelion: 1.0, cut no. 713
Still image

Evangelion: 1.0, cut no. 713
Layout
Hideaki Anno
Pencil on paper
26 × 37 cm (10¼ × 14⅝ in.)

Tokyo-3 is a machine that pretends to be a city – its sole purpose is to serve as a battlefield, a horizontal plain on which Evangelions and Angels collide and fight. Several buildings are labelled with tags that read 'Tokyo III', indicating that these are not the usual structures but are actually weapons.

Evangelion: 1.0, cut no. 821
Still image

Evangelion: 1.0, cut no. 821
Layout
Hideaki Anno
Pencil on paper
26 × 37 cm (10¼ × 14⅝ in.)

Anno places particular emphasis on the relative sizes of the attackers, the defenders and their battle arena. Both enemies and heroes are usually just tall enough so that their heads can be seen above the buildings. Here, the Angel is positioned in the city while the Evangelion is about to attack from the mountains.

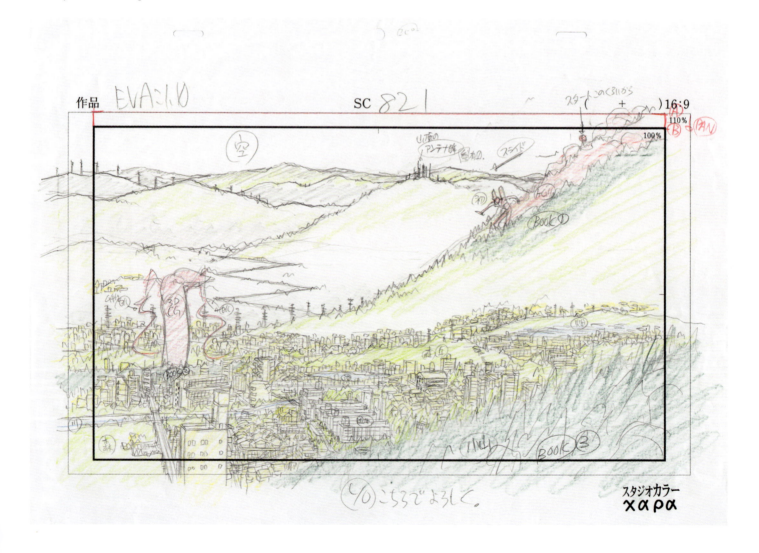

232 Rebuild of Evangelion

Evangelion: 1.0, cut no. 1184
Layout
Hideaki Anno
Pencil on paper
24 × 29.7 cm (9½ × 11¾ in.)

These structures have been lined up in a precise row so that the energy beam of an Angel can pass through them.

Evangelion: 1.0, cut no. 1184
Still image

Evangelion: 1.0, cut no. 1195
Still image

Evangelion: 1.0, cut no. 1195
Layout
Hideaki Anno
Pencil on paper
26 × 37 cm (10¼ × 14⅝ in.)

Behind a metal shield, the Evangelion rises in the middle of the street from its underground shelter.

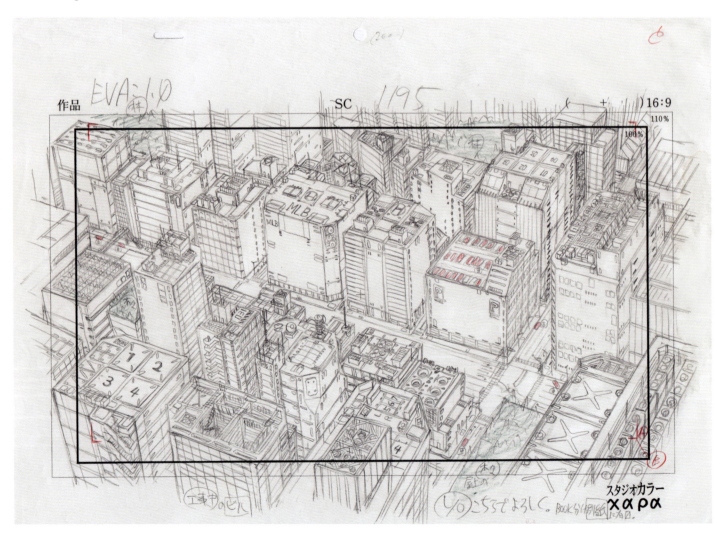

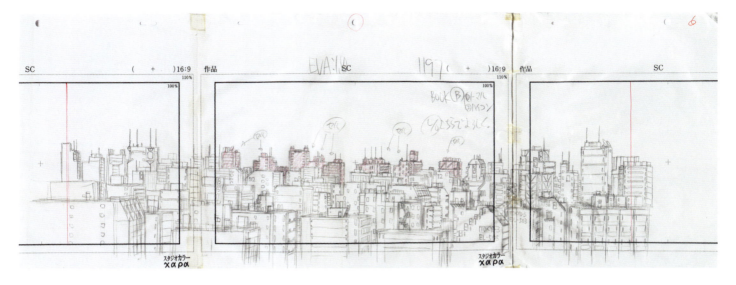

Evangelion: 1.0, cut no. 1197/1
Layout, foreground
Hideaki Anno
Pencil on paper
24 × 66 cm (9½ × 26 in.)

These layouts define the background and foreground of cut no. 1197. The camera moves from right to left across the image as the city suffers another blast from an attacking Angel. This cut is animated with a 2D technique – the two planes move at different speeds, creating the impression of depth as a result of the parallax effect. The crinkles are the consequence of the joining of separate sheets.

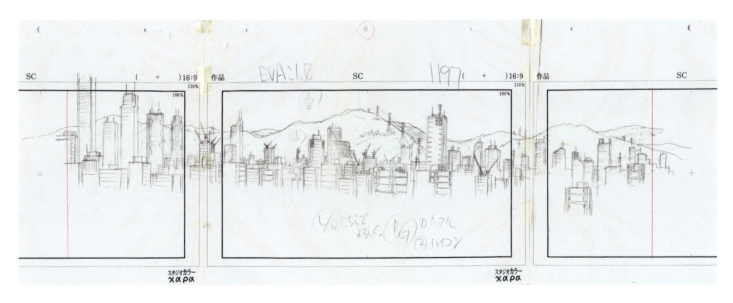

Evangelion: 1.0, cut no. 1197/2
Layout, background
Hideaki Anno
Pencil on paper
24 × 66 cm (9½ × 26 in.)

Evangelion: 1.0, cut no. 1197
Still image

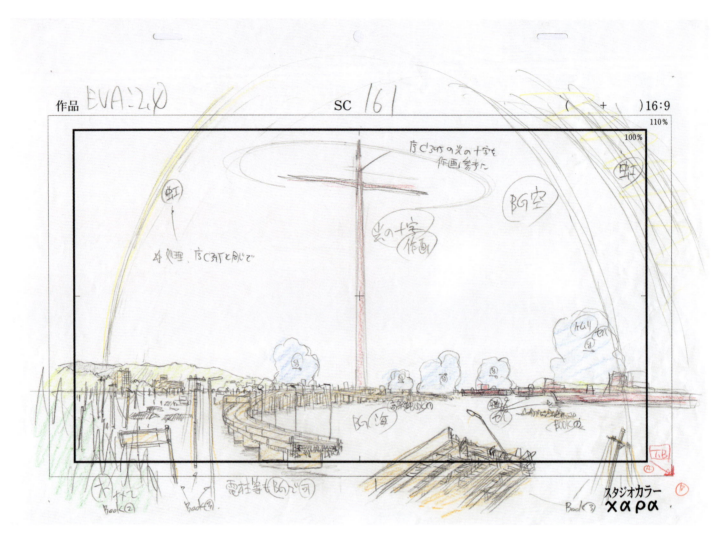

Evangelion: 2.0, cut no. 161
Layout
Hideaki Anno
Pencil on paper
26 × 37 cm (10¼ × 14⅝ in.)

As one of the Angels is defeated by an Evangelion, it explodes in a cross-shaped puff and releases a blood-coloured liquid. *Neon Genesis Evangelion* borrows many symbols from Christianity and Judaism. According to assistant director Kazuya Tsurumaki, such visual references were intended to give the series an interesting and 'exotic' feel, but the use of these symbols did not imply that a Christian interpretation should be applied to the film (Tsurumaki 2002).

Evangelion: 2.0, cut no. 161
Still image

The Angel explodes above a red sea.

Evangelion: 2.0, cut no. 516
Still image

Evangelion: 2.0, cut no. 516
Layout
Hideaki Anno
Pencil on paper
24 × 35.7 cm (9½ × 14⅛ in.)

Anno's layouts show a great commitment to the close depiction of electrical infrastructure. He has stated that he spent a great deal of time drawing electrical equipment for the *Rebuild of Evangelion* films. His brother-in-law worked in a power company, and pointed out that 'the electricity of anime had many mistakes', so Anno investigated the appearance of electrical infrastructure thoroughly and drew it as accurately as possible (Anno 2008, p. 462).

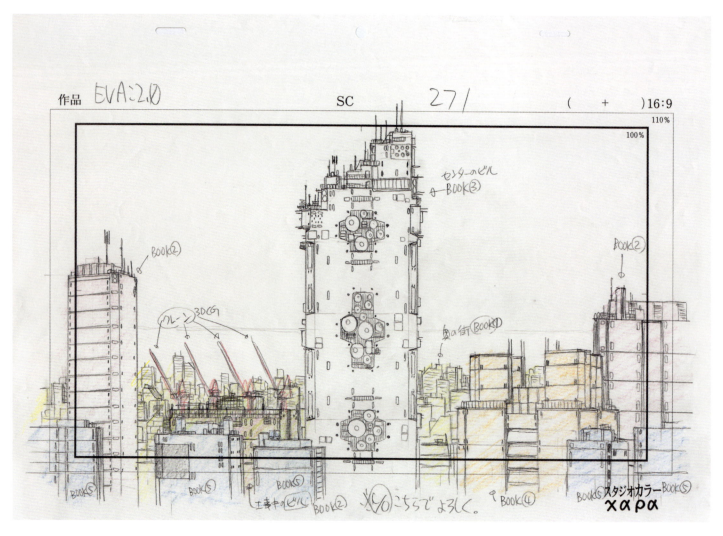

Evangelion: 2.0, cut no. 271
Layout
Hideaki Anno
Pencil on paper
26 × 37 cm (10¼ × 14⅝ in.)

A detailed depiction of one of the structures that is visible in the panoramic view of Tokyo-3 in cut no. 270 (see p. 225).

Evangelion: 2.0, cut no. 271
Still image

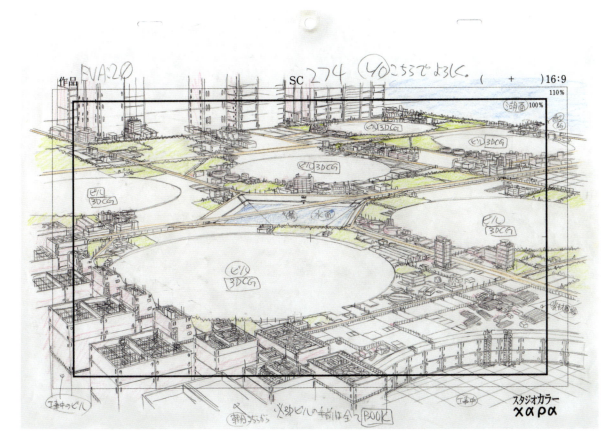

Evangelion: 2.0, cut no. 274
Layouts
Hideaki Anno
Pencil on paper
26 × 37 cm (10¼ × 14⅝ in.)

The layout above details the area around the base of the large solar-energy collectors in Tokyo-3 (see *Evangelion: 1.0*, cut no. 486 on p. 226). The round cut-outs where these collectors meet the ground are left empty, with a note specifying that these parts are to be realized in 3DCG. Instructions to the 3DCG department on their depiction are given in the layout to the right.

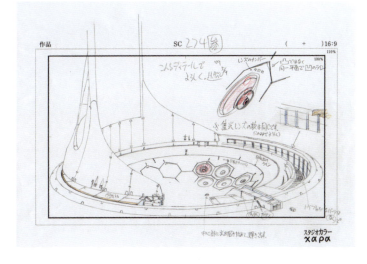

Evangelion: 2.0, cut no. 274
Still image

239

Takashi Watabe designed the 'Japan Marine Ecosystem Conservation Research Institute', a sea-water treatment plant that serves as the location for a major scene in *Evangelion: 2.0*. Anno's instructions were that a 'tree of life' form should act as the spine of this complex, from which huge living organs would spread out, symbolizing the purification of the sea water. As Watabe proceeded with the design, he found that a building with such a strange structure was an intriguing challenge, and it occurred to him that 'the entire complex is probably a creature made of machines' (Anno 2010, p. 174).

The basic design was laid out in CG. As Watabe drew more and more of the plant's elements, it became increasingly difficult to keep the proportions consistent. He believes that 'if it doesn't exist in reality, you can't go there and have a look', so he created the basic design using CG instead and, when this was finished, printed it out (the red lines on the sheet) before adding more details with pencil.

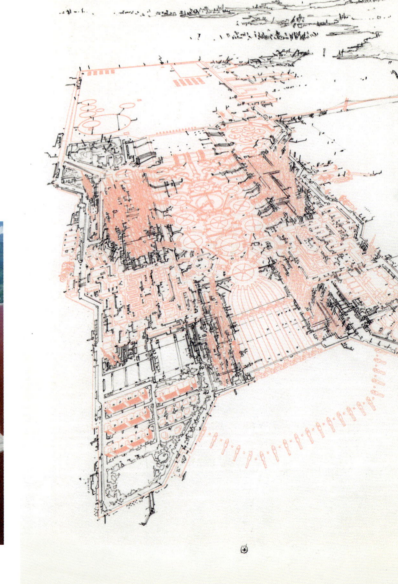

Evangelion: 2.0, cut no. 314
Art setting
Takashi Watabe
Pencil and printout on paper
29.7 × 21 cm (11¾ × 8⅜ in.)

Evangelion: 2.0, cut no. 314
Digital rendering

240 Rebuild of Evangelion

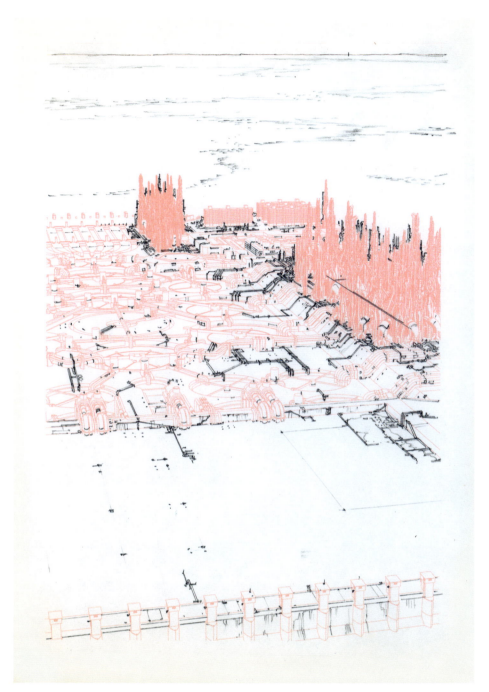

Evangelion: 2.0, cut no. 391
Art setting
Takashi Watabe
Pencil and printout on paper
29.7 × 21 cm (11¾ × 8⅜ in.)

Evangelion: 2.0, cut no. 391
Digital rendering

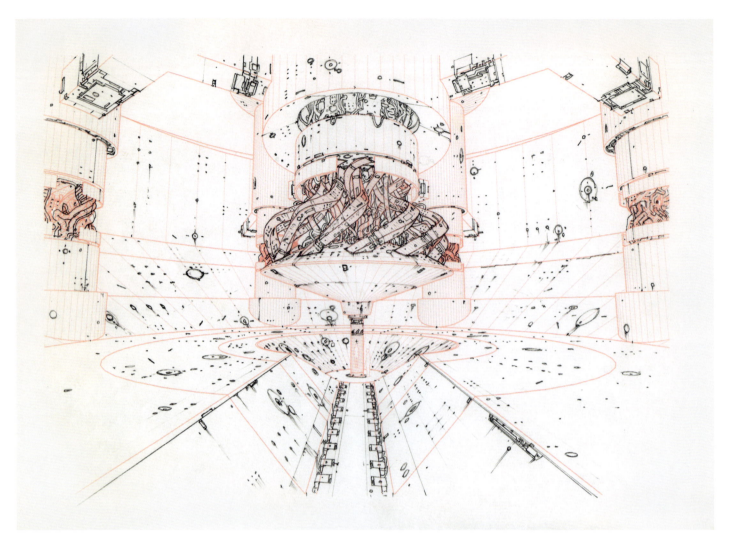

Evangelion: 2.0, cut no. 710
Art setting
Takashi Watabe
Pencil and printout on paper
21 × 29.7 cm (8⅜ × 11¾ in.)

Ayanami Rei, one of the three main characters in Neon Genesis Evangelion, is 'born' out of the cylindrical tank in the centre of this structure. Takashi Watabe first drew a series of rough sketches. He explains that 'the upper spiral structure is not filled with machinery, neither are the surrounding walls and pillars. These may contain organic tissue and living organisms' (Anno 2010, p. 103).

After the sketching phase, Watabe designed the entire space as a three-dimensional computer model to fix the camera perspective precisely. He then printed out this wireframe in red and added further detail in pencil. The drawing was scanned, the red lines replaced with black lines, and the whole layout was then processed digitally.

Evangelion: 2.0, cut no. 710
Still image

242 Rebuild of Evangelion

Evangelion: 2.0, cut no. 710
Rough sketches
Takashi Watabe
Pencil and printout on paper
17.6 × 25 cm (7 × 9⅞ in.)

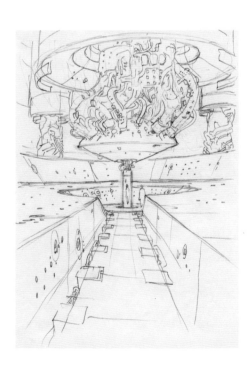
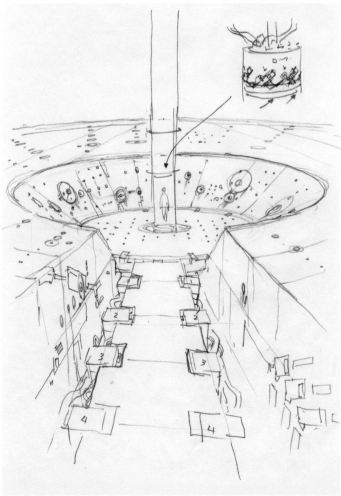

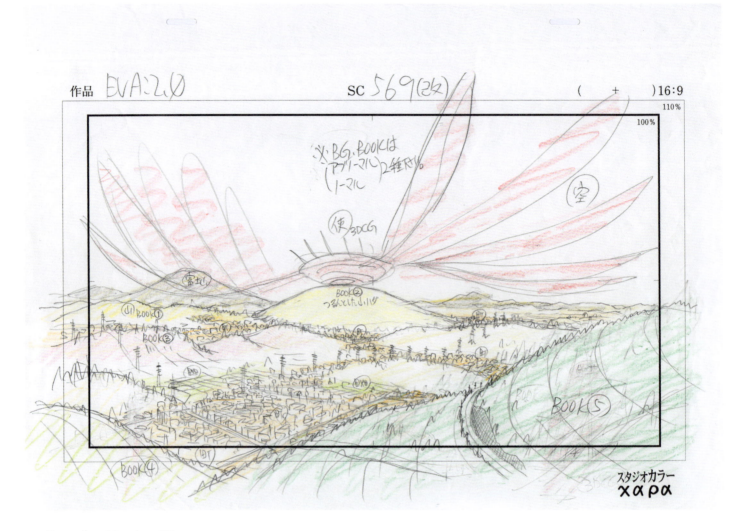

Evangelion: 2.0, cut no. 569
Layout
Hideaki Anno
Pencil on paper
26 × 37 cm (10¼ × 14⅝ in.)

The Eighth Angel settles on the top of a mountain near Tokyo-3. In this layout, the design of the alien being is based on Takashi Watabe's concepts.

Evangelion: 2.0, cut no. 569
Still image

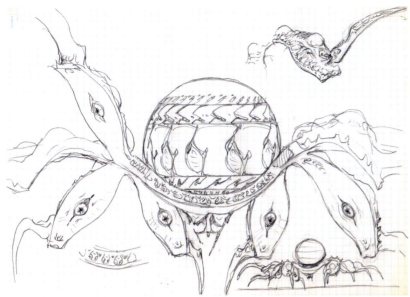

Evangelion: 2.0
Concept designs of the Eighth Angel
Takashi Watabe
Pencil on paper
21 × 29.7 cm (8 3/8 × 11 3/4 in.)

Watabe prepared concept designs for the Eighth Angel, but in the end his designs turned out to be 'too biological and were not suitable to be realized in CG' (Anno 2010, p. 264). Anno instead opted for something more 'geometrical, simple, and exciting'. The final design was executed by Masahiro Maeda.

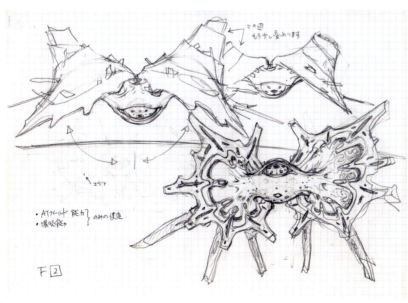

Evangelion: 2.0, cut no. 570
Still image

After the Eighth Angel is defeated (see p. 244), it releases a flood of red liquid that engulfs the city.

Evangelion: 2.0, cut no. 570
Layout
Hideaki Anno
Pencil on paper
26 × 37 cm (10¼ × 14⅝ in.)

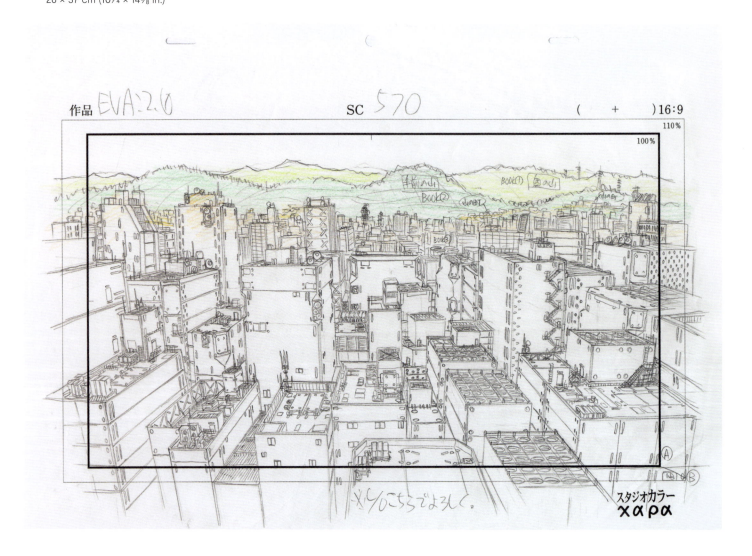

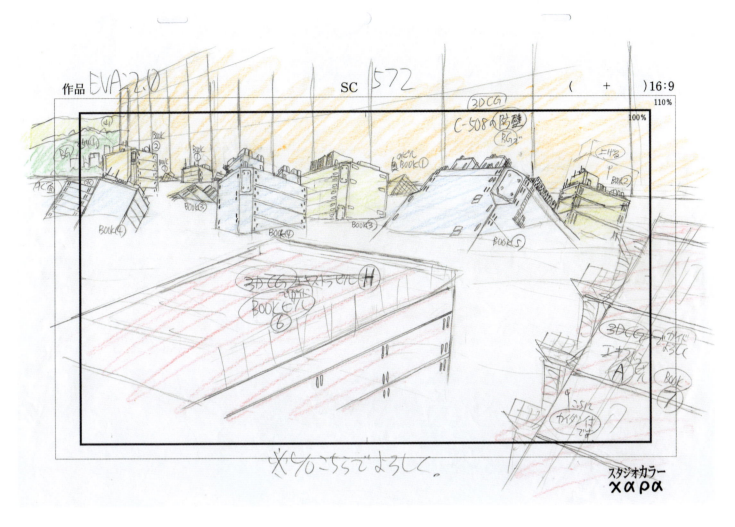

Evangelion: 2.0, cut no. 572
Layout
Hideaki Anno
Pencil on paper
26 × 37 cm (10¼ × 14⅝ in.)

As with all tokusatsu sets, Tokyo-3 is only built in order to be destroyed in the most compelling and spectacular manner. Ultimately, it has to be sacrificed for humanity to be saved once more.

Evangelion: 2.0, cut no. 572
Still image

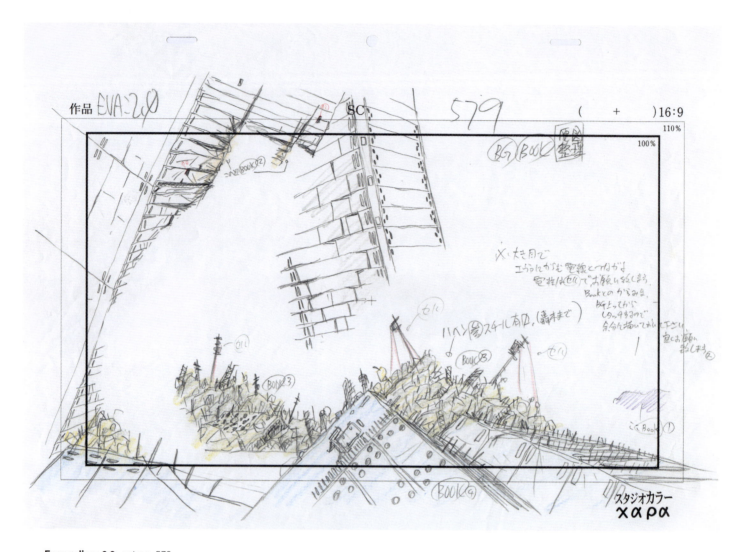

Evangelion: 2.0, cut no. 579
Layout
Hideaki Anno
Pencil on paper
26 × 37 cm (10¼ × 14⅝ in.)

The Evangelion that defeats the Angel winds up in a destroyed building. In this layout, its silhouette is visible as a white shadow. Annotations on the layout instruct the art department as follows: 'Please [draw] all power poles and electric wires on a cel. I [Anno] will retouch the parts that relate to the book after BG [background] is finished. Therefore, please draw [power poles] in surplus. Please start from here.'

Evangelion: 2.0, cut no. 579
Still image

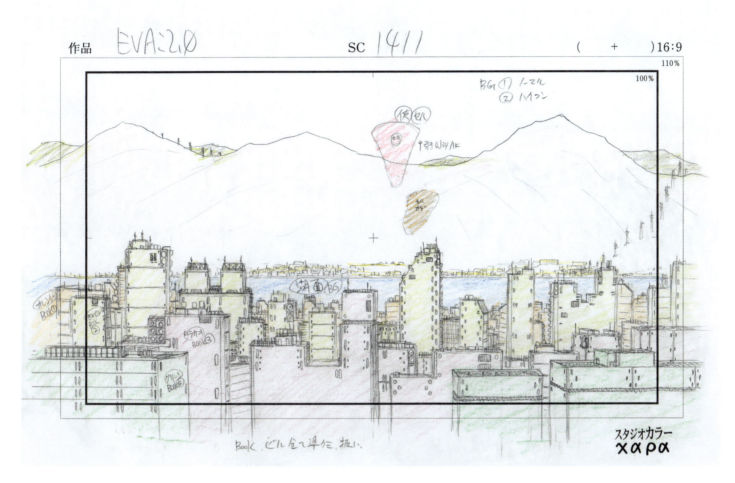

Evangelion: 2.0, cut no. 1411
Layout
Hideaki Anno
Pencil on paper
26 × 37 cm (10¼ × 14⅝ in.)

Another Angel appears on top of the mountains surrounding Tokyo-3 before the next battle scene commences.

Evangelion: 2.0, cut no. 1411
Still image

Glossary

Anime
General Japanese term for animated films; an abbreviation of the word 'animation'. In the West, the term is generally used to describe animated films produced in Japan. As elsewhere, the word is pronounced in Japanese in a manner that departs from normal linguistic rules. Consequently, as with some other Japanese words, anime is sometimes written as 'animé' to highlight this emphasis on its final letter. The word 'anime' usually appears either as a noun without a plural form, or as an adjective.

Art director
The art director of an anime production is responsible for the art department, overseeing the staff of background artists while also painting background artwork themselves. At an early phase of the production, the art director produces image boards. Image boards are initial drafts of production designs, and sometimes also of characters, that determine the basic look of the film, including colour palettes and lighting moods. Often the art director draws and paints detailed art settings and artboards with schematic backgrounds to make it clear to the background painters how the backgrounds are supposed to look. Finally, the art director usually supplies key elements of the artwork and draws backgrounds.

Background
The background is everything that appears in a picture behind the characters, and is the work of the art department under the art director – everything related to the characters is the work of the animation department under the animation director. In paper-based animation, the background picture is painted on paper with poster colour, following the guidance provided by the layout and image-board designs. The sheets of paper for the background usually have a larger format than the cels on which the figures are drawn to enable camera movements across the background. In more elaborate productions, the backgrounds also consist of several levels, thus creating a more complex production design.

Book cel
A book cel, or book for short, consists of several layers, some of them transparent (known as 'cels'), that make up the multi-layered structure of the film image. The individual layers are placed on top of one other in an analogue process using cels, or digitally through compositing. If a picture consists, for example, of background, middleground and foreground, the bottom layer will be painted on card and the middle and top layers on cels. These three layers together make up a book. In the case of figures, individual body parts may be put on different layers in a book in order to animate them. Camera effects such as depth-of-field blur can be created by moving the layers past the camera at different speeds and varying the distance between the individual layers. A book is also used when additional lighting effects are to be applied on an individual layer.

Cel
A transparent plastic sheet on which a part of an animation sequence is drawn. Cel is short for celluloid, the material from which the sheets are made. Cel technology was first patented in the USA in 1914 by Earl Hurd, and has played a major role in rationalizing the animation industry. Originally cellulose nitrate was used, which is highly inflammable, but this was later replaced by cellulose acetate. The decisive advantage of cel animation as opposed to other processes is that only the part of the picture that actually moves has to be repainted every time, whereas the static visual elements can remain on a sheet of paper under the cel for the duration of the cut.

Cut
In anime production, the editing is already finished in the storyboard phase. Therefore the term 'cut' does not refer to the transition between one shot and the next but to the images between two edits of the cinematic montage – the shot itself.

Frame
This term is used in two different ways. Firstly, it can mean the image's frame (or, in film terminology, the image field). On layouts, this frame is clearly visible as a black rectangle. The standard size of the frame in anime production is a '100', meaning one hundred per cent. Secondly, frame is also used to refer to the single film or animation image. An important related term is the frame rate. Film usually has an image rate of twenty-four frames per second, and most anime are shot 'on threes', meaning that an animation image depicting a phase of motion remains still for the duration of three recorded images – there are three image frames per drawing, so the frame rate is eight drawings per second.

Key frame
The animation of moving sequences is based on 'key frames' (Japanese: *genga*) and 'inbetweens' (Japanese: *doga*). The key frames of an animation define the start and end point, and are the most important phases in creating a smooth transition. They are refined by the insertion of additional frames called inbetweens into the sequence, until a fluid picture emerges. The key frames are drawn by specific 'key animators', and the inbetweens are drawn by 'inbetween animators'. The more inbetweens that are drawn, the more flowing the motion, and the more costly the production.

Layout
The layout is the separate construction sketch that is made for every image layer (background, middleground, foreground). It defines the essential characteristics of the shot, such as the picture construction and the framing. The layout is the most important drawing for the work of the background painters and key animators. If the camera moves over the background during a shot, the start and end points of the motion are specified in the layout. The corresponding camera framings are usually marked with red frames. The camera operator decides at what speed and acceleration the movement is eventually animated. Each layout is labelled with a scene and a cut number.

Location scout
The person who searches for specific locations for scenes. This is a regular position in the production crew for most live-action films, but for anime production the use of a location scout is rather unusual and may only be necessary when a high degree of realism is required.

Manga
General Japanese term for comics. Outside Japan, the term is used in most contexts to refer only to comics that originate from Japan.

Mecha
Derived from the word 'mechanical', this is a term used in science fiction to refer to giant piloted robots and robotic-type machines used for fighting. These usually take the form of humans, insects or birds. In the wider sense, mecha is also used to refer to technical items such as vehicles, machines and weapons. The mecha genre represents an important subcategory in science-fiction anime and manga.

Paper
The paper used for anime drawings is high-quality white or yellow paper with pre-punched holes on one side for alignment. The obverse side is smoother than the reverse side. The alignment holes are punched from the back. The paper has to be thin enough for the animator to be able to see through at least three layers when laying the sheets over each other on the lightbox. Layout paper is printed with the frame within which the layout should be drawn already in place.

Poster colour
Poster colours made by the Tokyo-based company Nicker are used by virtually every animation studio in Japan. Although these pigment-based paints are similar to watercolours in that they are water soluble and easy to spread, they are much more opaque. They dry with a matt finish, and are quite inexpensive compared to fine-art paints.

Set and setting
Set is the term for the location at which shooting takes place. In anime production, the set is designed by a concept designer. In science-fiction anime, the concept designer will also envision a completely fictitious world with its own laws and rules – the setting – that is both the location and the time period in which this story takes place.

Storyboard
The storyboard (Japanese: *e-konte*) is used to visualize the script, and is the first graphical representation of the cinematic storyline. It outlines the rough image sequence and includes the corresponding dialogue, as well as instructions for the animators.

Tokusatsu
Japanese term for live-action films or TV series that are distinguished by their considerable use of special effects created on set. The most popular examples of tokusatsu include monster films (Japanese: *kaiju eiga*) such as *Godzilla* (1954), directed by Ishiro Honda, and the superhero TV series *Ultraman* (1966–67), directed by Hajime Tsuburaya and Akio Jissoji.

Biographies

Hideaki Anno
Hideaki Anno (庵野秀明) was born in 1960 in Yamaguchi, and is an animator and director. He began his career after studying at the Osaka University of Arts. In 1983, he earned an immediate reputation by animating the God Warrior at the end of Hayao Miyazaki's *Nausicaa of the Valley of the Wind* (1984). He then produced his most famous work as an animator, the battle surrounding the rocket launch at the end of *Royal Space Force: The Wings of Honneamise* (1987), directed by Hiroyuki Yamaga. This was one of the first anime scenes that achieved a high degree of realism. In 1995, Anno directed all twenty-six episodes of the series *Neon Genesis Evangelion*, which is widely recognized as one of the most influential anime, and is the work with which his name is most associated. Anno particularly admires the films and effects of the tokusatsu genre (see p. 224). During the production of the *Rebuild of Evangelion* series (2007–), Anno has repeatedly stated that he wanted to create the special effects with a full-scale set, but could not do so because of budget constraints. In 2012, Anno wrote the script for the short film *Giant God Warrior Appears in Tokyo*, which was inspired by his original designs for *Nausicaa*'s God Warrior. This live-action short, directed by Shinji Higuchi and produced by Studio Ghibli, is a homage to tokusatsu, employing advanced special effects within its miniature set. In 2015, Anno and Higuchi co-directed *Shin Godzilla* (2016), the thirty-first instalment of the franchise that gave birth to the genre.

Michael Arias
Michael Arias was born in 1968 in Los Angeles, and works in live action, visual effects, computer graphics and anime. He started his career in 1987 at Dream Quest Images, working as a camera assistant on the motion-control stages of *The Abyss* (1989) and *Total Recall* (1990). In 1991, Arias moved to Tokyo to work at Imagica and Sega, after which he returned to the US to co-found effects boutique Syzygy Digital Cinema, before moving to CG company Softimage. There he developed and patented tools for combining traditional animation and computer graphics, working closely with Studio Ghibli to add a distinct visual flavour to Miyazaki's masterpieces *Princess Mononoke* (1997) and *Spirited Away* (2001). In 2000, Michael accepted an invitation from the Wachowski siblings and producer Joel Silver to produce the *Matrix*-inspired animated anthology *The Animatrix*, which won numerous awards. In 2006, following up on this success, Arias made his debut as a feature director with *Tekkonkinkreet*, shown at the Berlinale and awarded Japan's Academy Award for Best Animated Feature Film. In 2009, Arias directed *Heaven's Door*, his first live-action feature. Arias made his return to anime with the sci-fi thriller *Harmony* (co-directed with Takashi Nakamura) in 2015, and in 2018 directed live-action series *Tokyo Alien Bros* for Nippon Television.

Haruhiko Higami
Concept photographer Haruhiko Higami (樋上晴彦) was born in Saitama Prefecture. He studied economics at Gakushuin University in Tokyo, graduating in 1978. Higami was involved in documentary-film projects as a student. After his first job in a TV studio, he worked as a photographer at an advertising agency and at a photographic studio. In 1971, he started working as a product photographer for Popy, shooting toy figures. A subsidiary of Bandai Entertainment, Popy was a leading manufacturer of robot figures from 1971 to 1983. The toy industry is traditionally one of the largest sponsors of anime production, and this gave Higami his first contact with the anime scene. Since the mid-1980s, he has been a concept photographer and location scout for film and anime, working especially closely with the director Mamoru Oshii. The two men met during the shooting of Oshii's live-action film *The Red Spectacles* (1987), on which Higami worked as a stills photographer. It was Oshii who established the position of concept photographer as part of the creative team of an anime production for the first time for *Patlabor: The Movie* (1989). The role is similar to that of a location scout in live-action film. After their first collaboration, Higami went on to work as a concept photographer for Oshii's films *Patlabor 2: The Movie* (1993), *Ghost in the Shell* (1995) and *Innocence* (2004).

Shinji Kimura
Shinji Kimura (木村真二) was born 1962 in Saitama Prefecture, and is an anime director and art director. He started his career at Kobayashi Production in 1981. One of his first assignments was the background artwork for Osamu Dezaki's *Space Adventure Cobra* (1982) under the art direction of Toshiharu Mizutani. He also participated in the production of Mamoru Oshii's *Urusei Yatsura 2: Beautiful Dreamer* (1984). As an art director he debuted with *Project A-Ko* (1986). In 1988, he worked as a background painter on Hayao Miyazaki's *My Neighbor Totoro*. He is also a close collaborator with Katsuhiro Otomo, with whom he published the picture book *Hipira-kun* (Tokyo: Shufu-to-Seikatsu Sha, 2002). This project was realized during the production of Otomo's anime *Steamboy* (2004). For *Steamboy*, Kimura served as art director and had great influence on the design of the film's world view, as detailed in his book *The Art of Steamboy* (Tokyo: Kodansha, 2004). Kimura also worked as art director on Michael Arias's *Tekkonkinkreet* (2006), where he had a key role in establishing the cityscape and setting for the film. He recently served as art director for *Children of the Sea* (2019), directed by Ayumu Watanabe.

Shuichi Kusamori
Shuichi Kusamori (草森秀一), born in 1961 in Kanagawa Prefecture, is an art director. In many productions he is credited as Shuichi Hirata (平田秀一). After his marriage in 2012, he adopted the family name of his wife, Kusamori. He studied at the Tokyo Designer Gakuin College for two years before joining Studio SF for one year as an employee. Afterwards he began

working as a freelance illustrator. Kusamori worked as a background artist on Isao Takahata's *Grave of the Fireflies* (1988) under art director Nizo Yamamoto. With Production I.G, he worked on Mamoru Oshii's *Patlabor 2: The Movie* (1993) and *Ghost in the Shell* (1995). In 2006, he established his own company, Taro House, a two-person studio that he still runs with his wife today. He served as art director on Rintaro's *Metropolis* (2001), based on Osamu Tezuka's classic manga. His intricate texture work was an important pillar of Oshii's Cannes-nominated *Innocence* (2004), and of the Annecy-selected *XxxHolic: A Midsummer Night's Dream* (2005), directed by Tsutomu Mizushima. His latest works as an art director include the *Psycho Pass* series (2012) and movie (2015).

Toshiharu Mizutani
Toshiharu Mizutani (水谷利春) joined Kobayashi Production in 1972. In 1979, he worked in the art department for Hayao Miyazaki's *Lupin III: The Castle of Cagliostro*. He served as one of the art directors for Osamu Dezaki's *Space Adventure Cobra* (1982), with Shinji Kimura as part of his team. In 1983, he left Kobayashi to establish Studio Fuga with his colleagues Hiroshi Ono and Hiromasa Ogura, and was its director from 1983 to 1997. During that period, he served as the art director for Katsuhiro Otomo's *AKIRA* (1988). In 1997, Mizutani left Studio Fuga and established his own studio, Moon Flower, which he runs to this day. His most notable assignments as art director include films in the *Soreike! Anpanman* series in 2004 and 2006, and the 2007 film adaptation of the *Forest of Piano* manga series. From 2012, he was the art director for the *Little Busters!* anime series.

Hiromasa Ogura
Hiromasa Ogura (小倉宏昌), born 1954 in Tokyo, is an art director. He started working in animated film at Kobayashi Production in 1977. He worked on Osamu Dezaki's *Space Adventure Cobra* (1982) under the art direction of Toshiharu Mizutani, and painted backgrounds for Hayao Miyazaki's *Lupin III: The Castle of Cagliostro* (1979). In 1983, Ogura left Kobayashi and set up Studio Fuga with Hiroshi Ono and Toshiharu Mizutani. During that time he also served as an art director on *Royal Space Force: The Wings of Honneamise* (1987), directed by Hiroyuki Yamaga. Ogura has worked closely with Mamoru Oshii since 1987. Their first collaboration was the film *Twilight Q: Mystery File 538* (1987), on which Haruhiko Higami also worked. In 1988 he contributed several background paintings to Katsuhiro Otomo's *AKIRA* (1988). Ogura was the art director of *Patlabor: The Movie* (1989), *Patlabor 2: The Movie* (1993) and *Ghost in the Shell* (1995). His close attention to signs of weathering on buildings complemented Oshii's dystopian urban visions. From 1995 to 2007, he was head of the art department at Production I.G. He was the art director for Oshii's *Jin-Roh: The Wolf Brigade* (2000), as well as the series *FLCL* (2000) and *Last Exile* (2003). He also worked on the background artwork of *Innocence* (2004) under the art direction of Shuichi Kusamori.

In 2007, Ogura founded his own studio, Ogura Koubo. Since then he has directed the artwork for the TV series *Ghost Hound* (2007), *Black Butler* (2008), *Strike Witches* (2008) and *Sora no Otoshimono* (2009). In 2015, he supplied background artwork for episode nineteen of the TV series *Shirobako*. In this episode, he is featured as himself, underlining his importance in the anime industry. A selection of his artwork has been published in his book *Hikari to yami: Ogura Hiromasa gashu* (Tokyo: Tokuma Shoten, Studio Ghibli, 2004).

Hiroshi Ono
Hiroshi Ono (大野広司) was born in 1952 in Aichi Prefecture, and joined Kobayashi Production in 1977. In 1982 he debuted as art director for the anime series *Tonde Mon Pe*. In 1983, he set up Studio Fuga with Hiromasa Ogura and Toshiharu Mizutani. In 1988, Ono started working with Mizutani on the artwork of Katsuhiro Otomo's *AKIRA*, but then received a call from Studio Ghibli asking him to become the art director for Hayao Miyazaki's *Kiki's Delivery Service* (1989), an offer that he felt he could not reject. Since 1997, when Mizutani left, he has run Studio Fuga as its director. Ono directed the artwork for Hiroyuki Okiura's *A Letter to Momo* (2011) and Mamoru Hosoda's *Wolf Children* (2012). In 2015 he was responsible for the artwork of the award-winning *Miss Hokusai*, directed by Keiichi Hara (Annecy Jury Award). A selection of his artworks has been published in his book *Ono Kiroshi Background Art* (Tokyo: Kosaido, 2013).

Mamoru Oshii
Mamoru Oshii (押井守), born in 1951 in Tokyo, is one of Japan's leading film directors, active in both animation and live action, as well as television, computer games and manga. Oshii began making films as an arts education student at Tokyo Gakugei University. He joined Tatsunoko Productions (later renamed Production I.G) in 1977, and first worked as a director on the animated series *One-Hit Kanta*. In 1980, he moved to Studio Pierrot where he worked under Hisayuki Toriumi, who directed the series *The Wonderful Adventures of Nils* (1980–81), among many other projects. Oshii has been independent since 1984, and his many works have influenced such directors as James Cameron and the Wachowski siblings. His major works for the screen include *Urusei Yatsura: Only You* (director, film adaptation, storyboards; 1983); *Patlabor: The Movie* (director; 1989); *Patlabor 2: The Movie* (director; 1993); *Ghost in the Shell* (director; 1995); *Avalon* (director; 2001); *Innocence* (screenplay, director; 2004); and *The Sky Crawlers* (director; 2009).

Katsuhiro Otomo
Katsuhiro Otomo (大友克洋), born in 1954 in Miyagi Prefecture, is a manga artist, screenwriter and film director. In 1979, Otomo created his first science-fiction manga, *Fireball*. Although it was never completed, it was a milestone in Otomo's career as it contained many of the themes he explored in later works. In 1983, he made his anime debut, working as character designer for the animated film

Harmagedon: Genma Wars, directed by Rintaro. He then began work on his most acclaimed and best-known manga, *AKIRA*. It took him eight years to complete, consisting of 2,000 pages of artwork. In 1987, Otomo continued his work in anime, writing the screenplay for and directing a segment of the anthology *Neo Tokyo*. That same year he created two segments in another anthology, *Robot Carnival*. While the manga *AKIRA* was still being serialized, Otomo was asked to transform it into an animated feature film. Released in 1988, the film was a milestone in the international recognition of anime. As a screenwriter, Otomo also adapted Osamu Tezuka's manga *Metropolis* (1949) for the anime of the same name directed by Rintaro and released in 2001. After ten years of production, his own feature-length film *Steamboy* was released in 2004, and at the time was the most expensive anime production ever made. *Steamboy* was produced by studio Sunrise, as was his 2006 mini-series *Freedom Project*. In 2013, Otomo released the anthology *Short Peace*, which consists of four shorts. His latest feature film, *Orbital Era*, is scheduled for release in 2020.

Atsushi Takeuchi

Atsushi Takeuchi (竹内 敦志) was born in 1965 in Fukuoka Prefecture, and entered the anime industry as an aspiring mechanical designer. His skill in the realistic depiction of mechanical elements and his sensitivity towards complex layouts during the production of Mamoru Oshii's *Patlabor: The Movie* (1989) won him a position among the main staff on Oshii's subsequent works. Since then, Takeuchi has maintained a close relationship with both Oshii and Production I.G, working on the layouts and the mechanical design for *Patlabor 2: The Movie* (1993), *Ghost in the Shell* (1995) and *Innocence* (2004). In recent years, he has expanded his field of activities to production and direction. As the guest director for the tenth episode of the TV series *Star Wars: The Clone Wars* (2008), Takeuchi was the first Japanese director to handle part of the Star Wars cinematic universe.

Takashi Watabe

Takashi Watabe (渡部 隆), born in 1959, is a concept designer, mechanical designer and layout designer. He lives in Niigata in northern Japan. Before working in the anime industry, he studied design and researched descriptive geometry at the visual-design department of Tokyo Zokei University. His drafts for production design, buildings and mechanical elements such as vehicles and robots are the conceptual basis for the overall world views of many anime. In 1987, Watabe oversaw the layout work for *Royal Space Force: The Wings of Honneamise*, directed by Hiroyuki Yamaga. His designs impressed the creative personnel involved, establishing his reputation in the scene. The film was produced by Studio Gainax and was the first full-length anime feature rendered in the meticulous realistic style that would later become the hallmark of Japanese animated films. Hideaki Anno and Hiromasa Ogura also worked on this production. Since then, Watabe has worked with numerous studios and many of the most influential directors, including almost every production featured in this publication. His projects include *Nausicaa of the Valley of the Wind* (assistant key animator; 1984); *Neo Tokyo: The Running Man* (mecha design; 1987); *AKIRA* (layout; 1988); *Patlabor: The Movie* (layout; 1989); *Patlabor 2: The Movie* (layout; 1993); *Ghost in the Shell* (layout, production design, background design; 1995); *Metropolis* (layout; 2001); *Innocence* (layout; 2004); *XxxHolic: A Midsummer Night's Dream* (production design; 2005); *Freedom Project* (concept design; 2006); *Evangelion: 1.0 You Are (Not) Alone* (concept design; 2007); *The Sky Crawlers* (layout, production design; 2008); *Evangelion: 2.0 You Can (Not) Advance* (layout, production design; 2009); *009: ReCyborg* (art setting, layout; 2012); *Evangelion: 3.0 You Can (Not) Redo* (concept design; 2012); *Ghost in the Shell: The New Movie* (art settings; 2015); and *Garm Wars: The Last Druid* (mecha design; 2015).

About the Author

Stefan Riekeles is a curator based in Berlin. He holds a master's degree in Culture Studies and Audio Communication Science from the Humboldt University and the Technical University in Berlin. He has been the Artistic Director of the Japan Media Arts Festival Dortmund, and curated the exhibition 'Proto Anime Cut' which toured from 2011 until 2013. He served as the Programme Director of the International Symposium on Electronic Art 2010 and curated exhibitions for transmediale festival for art and digital culture in Berlin. Riekeles is the vice chairman of Les Jardins des Pilotes, Berlin.

References

Anno, H. (2007), *Rebuild of Evangelion: 1.0 You Are (Not) Alone* (film), Tokyo: Khara.

Anno, H. (2008), *Rebuild of Evangelion: 1.0 You Are (Not) Alone, Complete Record* (book), Tokyo: Khara.

Anno, H. (2009), *Rebuild of Evangelion: 2.0 You Can (Not) Advance* (film), Tokyo: Khara.

Anno, H. (2010), *Rebuild of Evangelion: 2.0 You Can (Not) Advance, Complete Record* (book), Tokyo: Khara.

Arias, M. (2004), *Tekkonkinkreet Director's Notes*, retrieved from http://michaelarias.net.

Arias, M. & Tanaka, E. & Studio 4°C (2006), *Tekkonkinkreet* (film), Tokyo: Aniplex.

Clements, J. & McCarthy, H. (2015), *The Anime Encyclopedia: A Century of Japanese Animation*, (book: 3rd ed.), New York: Stone Bridge Press.

Kimura, S. (2006a), *Tekkonkinkreet Art Book: Shiro Side* (book), Tokyo: Beyond C.

Kimura, S. (2006b), *Tekkonkinkreet Art Book: Kuro Side* (book), Tokyo: Beyond C.

Les Jardins des Pilotes (2011–13), 'Proto Anime Cut' (exhibition): Künstlerhaus Bethanien, Berlin (21 January – 6 March 2011); HMKV im Dortmunder U, Dortmund (9 July – 9 October 2011); Espai Cultural de Caja Madrid, Barcelona (8 February – 8 April 2012); La Casa Encendida, Madrid (5 July – 16 September 2012); Kumu Art Museum of Estonia, Tallinn (7 February – 19 May 2013); Cartoonmuseum Basel (8 June – 13 October 2013).

Les Jardins des Pilotes (2016–), 'Anime Architecture' (exhibition): Tchoban Foundation – Museum for Architectural Drawing, Berlin (23 July – 16 October 2016); House of Illustration, London (27 May – 10 September 2017); Japan Foundation, Sydney (1 June – 11 August 2018); Gosford Regional Gallery, Gosford (30 March – 10 May 2019); Morikami Museum and Japanese Gardens, Delray Beach, Florida (9 November 2019 – 3 April 2020).

Mead, S., Hodgetts, C. & Villeneuve, D. (2017), *The Movie Art of Syd Mead: Visual Futurist* (book), London: Titan Books.

Ogura, H. (2004), *Hikari to yami: Ogura Hiromasa gashu* (book), Tokyo: Tokuma Shoten, Studio Ghibli.

Oshii, M. & Ito, K. (1989), *Patlabor: The Movie* (film), Tokyo: Bandai Visual Co., Ltd.

Oshii, M. (1993a), *Patlabor 2: The Movie* (film), Tokyo: Bandai Visual Co., Ltd, Tohokushinsha Film Corporation, Production I.G & Headgear.

Oshii, M. (1993b), *Patlabor 2: The Movie Archives* (book), Tokyo: Bandai Visual Co., Ltd, Tohokushinsha Film Corporation & Production I.G.

Oshii, M., Kubo, M. & Nozaki, T. (1994), *Methods: Layouts of Patlabor 2: The Movie* (book), Tokyo: Kadokawa Shoten.

Oshii, M. & Shirow, M. (1995a), *Ghost in the Shell* (film), Tokyo: Kodansha.

Oshii, M. & Shirow, M. (1995b), *The Analysis of Ghost in the Shell* (book), Tokyo: Kodansha.

Oshii, M., Mitsuhisa, I., Suzuki, T., Shirow, M. & Production I.G (2004a), *Innocence* (film), Japan: Production I.G.

Oshii, M. (2004b), *Innocence: The Official Art Book* (book), Tokyo: Tokuma Shoten.

Oshii, M. & Production I.G (2005), *Methods: From Layouts of Innocence* (book), Tokyo: Kadokawa Shoten.

Otomo, K. (1984), *AKIRA* (graphic novel), Tokyo: Mash Room Co., Ltd (first published from 1982 by *Young Magazine*, Tokyo: Kodansha Ltd).

Otomo, K. (1988), *AKIRA* (film), Tokyo: Mash Room Co., Ltd, AKIRA Committee. Based on the manga *AKIRA* by Katsuhiro Otomo, first published from 1982 by *Young Magazine*, Tokyo: Kodansha Ltd.

Otomo, K. (1989), *AKIRA: Production Report* (DVD extra), Tokyo: AKIRA Committee.

Otomo, K. (2002), *AKIRA Animation Archives* (book), Tokyo: Kodansha.

Riekeles, S. (2011), *Proto Anime Cut Archive: Spaces and Vision in Japanese Animation* (book), Heidelberg: Kehrer.

Tsurumaki, K. (2002), interview, retrieved from http://www.tomodachi.de.

Image credits

Need Kajima: pp. 6, 10, 14–15
Illustration: Shuichi Kusamori (Production I.G, Inc.)
© 2007 Shuichi Kusamori / Production I.G

AKIRA: pp. 18–55
Based on the graphic novel *AKIRA* by Katsuhiro Otomo.
First published by *Young Magazine*, Kodansha Ltd.
© 1988 MASH · ROOM / AKIRA COMMITTEE
All Rights Reserved

Patlabor: The Movie: pp. 56–67
© 1989 Headgear

Patlabor 2: The Movie: pp. 68–91
© 1993 Headgear

Ghost in the Shell: pp. 92–135
© 1995 Shirow Masamune / KODANSHA ·
BANDAI VISUAL · MANGA ENTERTAINMENT.
All Rights Reserved

Metropolis: pp. 136–57
© 2001 TEZUKA PRODUCTIONS / METROPOLIS
COMMITTEE. Licensed from BANDAI NAMCO
Arts Inc. All Rights Reserved

Innocence: pp. 158–85
© 2004 Shirow Masamune / Kodansha · Production I.G

Tekkonkinkreet: pp. 186–221
© 2006 Taiyo Matsumoto / Shogakukan, Aniplex,
Asmik Ace, Beyond C, Dentsu, TOKYO MX

*Rebuild of Evangelion: 1.0 You Are (Not) Alone /
Rebuild of Evangelion: 2.0 You Can (Not) Advance*:
pp. 222–49
© 2007–2009 Hideaki Anno / Khara

The research for this publication was generously
supported by Les Jardins des Pilotes e.V. für Kunst und
Kultur, Berlin, Germany.

les jardins des pilotes

On the cover:
Front – ©1988 MASH · ROOM / AKIRA COMMITTEE.
All Rights Reserved. Based on the graphic novel
AKIRA by Katsuhiro Otomo. First published by *Young
Magazine*, Kodansha Ltd.
Back – ©2001 TEZUKA PRODUCTIONS /
METROPOLIS COMMITTEE. Licensed from BANDAI
NAMCO Arts Inc. All Rights Reserved.

First published in the United Kingdom in 2020
by Thames & Hudson Ltd, 181A High Holborn,
London WC1V 7XQ

First published in the United States of America in 2020
by Thames & Hudson Inc., 500 Fifth Avenue, New York,
New York 10110

Reprinted 2022

*Anime Architecture: Imagined Worlds and Endless
Megacities* © 2020 Thames & Hudson Ltd, London

Text © 2020 Stefan Riekeles
Design by Praline
Production Assistant Hiroko Myokam

All Rights Reserved. No part of this publication may
be reproduced or transmitted in any form or by any
means, electronic or mechanical, including photocopy,
recording or any other information storage and
retrieval system, without prior permission in writing
from the publisher.

British Library Cataloguing-in-Publication Data
A catalogue record for this book is available from
the British Library

Library of Congress Control Number 2020931749

ISBN 978-0-500-29452-9

Printed and bound in China by
Artron Art (Group) Co., Ltd

Be the first to know about our new releases,
exclusive content and author events by visiting
thamesandhudson.com
thamesandhudsonusa.com
thamesandhudson.com.au